G⦿D
SAVE
THE
KI⦿NG

The Sacred Nature
of the Monarchy

IAN BRADLEY

DARTON · LONGMAN + TODD

First published in 2023 by
Darton, Longman and Todd Ltd
1 Spencer Court
140 – 142 Wandsworth High Street
London SW18 4JJ

© 2023 Ian Bradley

The right of Ian Bradley to be identified as the Author
of this work has been asserted in accordance with the
Copyright, Designs and patents Act 1988.

ISBN: 978-1-915412-52-2

A catalogue record for this book is available from the British
Library.

Printed and bound in Great Britain by
Short Run Press, Exeter

This book is dedicated to all those involved in the planning of King Charles III's coronation, code-named 'Operation Golden Orb' in recognition, I hope and trust, of its sacred character.

CONTENTS

INTRODUCTION

Interviewing me about the accession of King Charles III to the United Kingdom throne following the death of his mother, Queen Elizabeth II, in September 2022, a distinguished columnist from the *Washington Post* expressed his astonishment about one particular aspect of the process: 'For a country which is so secular and where so few go to church, you sure mention God a lot.' He is absolutely right. The official ceremonies that mark the accession of a new monarch are steeped in religious language. The Proclamation of Accession, read out at St James's Palace, London, in Edinburgh, Cardiff and Hillsborough and in cities and towns across the nation began: 'Whereas it has pleased Almighty God to call to His Mercy our late Sovereign Lady Queen Elizabeth the Second' and went on to note that Charles III rules 'by the Grace of God' and to beseech 'God, by whom kings and queens do reign, to bless His Majesty with long and happy Years to reign over us'. In similar terms, the new king spoke of his reliance on God's help in every one of his public speeches following his accession and the Almighty was invoked by most of the political leaders offering condolences and delivering loyal addresses in the parliaments and assemblies of the United Kingdom. God is, of course, directly referenced on every coin of the realm where the abbreviations *D. G. Rex* and *F.D.* (sometimes extended to *Fid Def*) signify that the king (*Rex*) rules by the grace of God (*Dei Gratia*) and is Defender of the Faith (*Fide Defensor*).

My American interrogator will be even more bemused by the overtly religious atmosphere of the coronation at which Charles will be formally invested with regal authority. It is a service of Christian worship, traditionally framed in the context of a celebration of Holy Communion and directly modelled on the crowning of Israelite kings as described in the Hebrew Bible, in which the new monarch is anointed with holy oil, consecrated and set apart in the manner of a priestly ordination. The coronation oaths, which perhaps come nearer than anything else to expressing the essence of the unwritten British constitution, are also markedly and explicitly Christian in character, binding the new monarch to 'maintain the Laws of God and the true profession of the Gospel' and more explicitly to 'maintain in the United Kingdom the Protestant Reformed Religion' and to preserve inviolably 'the settlement of the Church of England, and the doctrine, worship, discipline and government thereof'. The first official utterance by Charles as king at the Accession Council held just two days after his mother's death, made with the Bible in his right hand, was an oath in which he solemnly swore to maintain the Presbyterian government of the Church of Scotland.

The fact is that although we may not 'do God' in Britain in the manner of American politicians who conclude every speech with the words 'God bless America', our unwritten constitution is undergirded by a sense of divine providence and guidance and an understanding that we owe our ultimate allegiance to something greater than ourselves. This God language is focused around the monarchy which in our profoundly secular and supposedly post-Christian nation is still surrounded by religious imagery and symbolism and remains perhaps the one institution with a clear Christian focus, not least in its intimate relationship with and responsibility for maintaining and preserving the doctrine, worship and government of the country's two established churches.

More than four hundred years ago William Shakespeare was similarly struck that 'such Divinity should hedge a king'. The public mood has changed considerably since he gave that line to Claudius in *Hamlet*. Few if any now believe in the theory of the Divine Right of Kings which many subscribed to in the seventeenth century, or indeed take the view that polls suggest was still held by two thirds of the British population at the time of the last coronation in 1953, that the monarch is directly chosen by God. Yet quite apart from the frequent referencing of what has been described as 'the transcendent God of the state occasion' in connection with the institution of monarchy, there is still a widespread popular appreciation of and identification with the monarchy's spiritual and religious aura, expressed in more immanent and intimate terms.

This was underlined by the public reaction to the death of Queen Elizabeth II. Commentators were struck by the very large numbers of people who turned out to witness the progress of the Queen's coffin from Balmoral to Edinburgh, to file past it in the High Kirk of St Giles and Westminster Hall and to line the streets for its final journey from London to Windsor. What struck me was how many of them bowed, knelt or crossed themselves, using essentially religious gestures and rituals. Many of those interviewed described seeing the coffin, even if only passing by in a hearse, as a spiritual experience. The proprietor of a tourist souvenir shop along Edinburgh's Royal Mile, which remained largely unvisited in the hours before, during and after the passage of the coffin from the Palace of Holyrood to St Giles, summed up the atmosphere in the city centre as 'sacred'.

There was, indeed, something very medieval and very Catholic about the enormous respect, amounting almost to veneration, shown towards the late queen's corporeal remains in their lead lined oak coffin. Several of those patiently waiting for up to 24 hours in the queue to file past the coffin in Westminster Hall, which at one point stretched to ten miles, described it as being like a pilgrimage. One of the volunteer chaplains to the queue told me that he had several requests for prayer and was even asked to bless a ten month old baby who was being taken by her grandmother to pay her respects. Ironically, given the monarchy's role as protector of Protestantism, indeed arguably the last great bastion of Protestant Britain, there was more than a hint of the cult of saints' relics, reinforced by the spontaneous creation of shrines around the gates of the royal palaces made up of votive offerings in the form of flowers, Paddington Bear figures and marmalade sandwiches. People seemed to feel a need to be close to the late Queen's body – even though in Christian understanding her soul had long departed – just as many sought to reach out and shake the hands of the new King, his Queen Consort and the new Prince and Princess of Wales on their walkabouts in gestures which recalled the medieval and early modern practice of touching for the king's evil.

In addition to those who sought some kind of physical contact with either the departed or the new monarch, many more went to churches and cathedrals to express their grief and pray for the new reign. Birmingham Cathedral alone had 10,000 visitors in the three days following the Queen's death and Wakefield Cathedral became a mecca for Muslim families who welcomed the opportunity to light a candle. Churches provided a place and a space for grieving, contemplation and reflection on the part of the great unchurched majority of the nation and for adherents of minority faiths.

In an article in *The Times* which attracted a good deal of attention, I argued that both the official events and the popular reaction following the death of Queen Elizabeth II and the accession of King Charles III perhaps revealed Britain to be a more religious country than statistics of decline in churchgoing and sociological studies of secularisation might suggest. They had, I suggested, 'underlined and uncovered a deep residual spiritual strain, explicitly though not exclusively Christian, at the heart of the nation'. I went on to say that 'What we have witnessed is the resurgence of a long latent and never quite dormant implicit folk religion which is emotional and instinctive rather than rational or intellectual. It is expressed in feeling more than in believing and it is not exclusively Christian – indeed it finds moving expression by adherents of other faiths.'[1]

It is not surprising that it should be the monarchy that unleashed this latent spirituality and religious sentiment which usually lies hidden. It is perhaps the one institution left in the country with the power and capacity still to evoke a popular religious response, explicitly though not exclusively Christian. More than 150 years ago Walter Bagehot, the Victorian essayist, noted that the monarchy constitutes 'the solitary transcendent element in the state' which 'strengthens our government with the strength of religion'.[2] Nor is it surprising that for many people encounters with royalty often take on the character of a religious experience and that words like 'reverence', 'grace' and 'blessing' are commonly used to describe them. This struck the American travel writer Paul Theroux while journeying round Britain in the early 1980s. Arriving in the coastal town of Anstruther in Fife just after it had been visited by Queen Elizabeth II, he noted that 'It was as if the town had been refreshed with a blessing. In a way it had, for that atmosphere was the spirit left by the progress of the Royal visit.'[3] The social anthropologist, Anne Rowbottom, has shown just how strong a religious element there still is in the continuing love-affair between the majority of the British population and royalty. For her, the ultimate ground of pro-royal sentiment is comparable with a religious force rather than with showbusiness or celebrity appeal.[4] For this reason, and for others as well, I believe that we can justifiably continue to apply to the monarchy the epithet 'sacred'.

This book, which is published to coincide with the coronation of King Charles III on 6 May 2023, is about the sacred nature of monarchy, and more specifically about its Christian character in the United Kingdom. To some extent, it echoes the theme of a series of sermons on the spiritual significance of the institution of monarchy preached by Geoffrey Fisher, the Archbishop of Canterbury, in the weeks leading up to the last coronation in 1953. He argued that reduced temporal power actually enhanced rather than diminished the importance of this aspect of monarchy, bringing about 'the possibility of a spiritual power far more exalted and far more searching in its demands: the power to lead, to inspire, to unite, by the Sovereign's personal character, personal convictions and personal example.'[5]

Throughout the seventy years of her reign Queen Elizabeth II supremely exemplified that spiritual power and calling of monarchy. It would be hard to think of any head of state in the world who more consistently and faithfully embodied the principle of selfless, even sacrificial, devotion to duty. Guided by a firm conviction in her calling and anointing by God, she represented and articulated the spiritual feelings of her people in the most solemn and consecrated moments of the nation's life. Although naturally reserved and undemonstrative over what she rightly regarded as a personal matter, she made no secret of her own strong Christian faith and her belief in the positive reconciling power of religion as a force for good and in the continuing validity of the teachings of the world's major faiths. In a period that saw a sea change in so many aspects of morality and culture, she stood as an exemplar of probity, decency and incorruptibility while in other respects moving with the times and never appearing stuffy or censorious. She gave one of the clearest indications of the nature as well as the depth of her Christian faith in her Christmas broadcast in 2014 when, after describing Jesus Christ as 'an inspiration and an anchor in my life', she went on to enumerate his most distinctive attributes as 'reconciliation, forgiveness, love, acceptance and healing' (see page 202).

King Charles III has already made a notable contribution to the religious life of Britain with his consistent call during his long royal apprenticeship as Prince of Wales for more emphasis to be given to the spiritual and holistic dimension of life, his particular interest in Islam and inter-faith dialogue, which bore practical fruit in the Respect for Faith initiative, and his passionate championship of causes ranging from the Book of Common Prayer to sacred geometry. These and other themes were brought together in his book *Harmony: A New Way of Looking at Our World*, which mounted a powerful attack on post-Enlightenment modernism, materialism and rationalism and argued for the innate harmony and deep interconnectedness of all things and for the re-enchantment of humanity through a greater sense of the sacred, a re-connection with the beauty and spirit of nature and a deeper awareness of the presence of God. In his first address to the nation as king, he spoke of 'the sovereign's particular relationship and responsibility towards the Church of England, the church in which my own faith is so deeply rooted' and went on to say, 'in that faith, and the values it inspires, I have been brought up to cherish a sense of duty to others, and hold in the greatest respect the precious traditions, freedoms and responsibilities of our unique history and our system of parliamentary government.' In a subsequent speech in Buckingham Palace to leaders of all major faiths, he further declared, 'I am a committed Anglican Christian' and to say that 'as a member of the Church of England, my Christian beliefs have love at their very heart'.

This book explores the archetype of sacred

kingship, its origins in primal religion, its central role in both the Old and New Testaments of the Bible and its representation in modern popular culture. It charts the development of Christian monarchy in the history of the British Isles and describes the significance and symbolism of the coronation. It also analyses the relationship between sovereign and church, the monarch's traditional roles as protector of Protestantism and Defender of the Faith and how these are being reinterpreted in the context of a multi-faith and multi-cultural Britain. The sacred engagements in the annual royal calendar are detailed, including such little-known rituals as the Christmas rose cut from the Glastonbury Thorn bush and the offering of the King's gifts at the Feast of the Epiphany. In essence, this book is both a celebration and an exploration of sacred monarchy as it has been understood and practised over the centuries and of its continuing relevance today.

Although the pages that follow focus primarily on the institution of monarchy, there is inevitably also consideration of the beliefs and practices of individual kings and queens. Christian monarchy involves duty and sacrificial service on the part of rulers as much as loyalty on the part of their subjects. It is about the example that monarchs set as disciples of Christ, the servant king. With this in mind, it is worth giving a brief tally of some of the contributions that have been made to Christian life and witness in the British Isles by our kings and queens. Westminster Abbey was the brainchild of Edward the Confessor and was rebuilt and enlarged by Henry III. St George's Chapel, Windsor, was built on the initiative of Edward III and Dunfermline Abbey by David I of Scotland. The first English Prayer Book owed much to Edward VI's personal support of Thomas Cranmer. The Authorised Version of the Bible came out of the Hampton Court Conference convened by James VI of Scotland and I of England. The king took a strong personal interest in the making of the Bible which he saw as an *irenicon*, an instrument of peace to bring together both the divided factions in the church and the nations of Scotland and England into a single United Kingdom. The practice of standing for the Hallelujah chorus in Handel's Messiah was begun by George III who rose to his feet during its first London performance in 1743. The entire audience followed his example, initiating a tradition that has continued ever since.

In a slightly less direct way, both of the established churches in the United Kingdom owe their status to the monarchy. The Church of England, indeed, owes its very existence to Henry VIII's determination to have a male heir, which precipitated his marriage to Anne Boleyn when he was already married to Catherine of Aragon, leading to his excommunication by the Pope. In the words of Stephen Bates in his recent book, *The Shortest History of the Crown*, 'Henry's bid to marry Anne Boleyn inadvertently led to the creation of a new Christian denomination, which would eventually become the Church of England.'[6] The Presbyterian Church of Scotland owes its establishment status to the fact that it supported William of Orange and his wife Mary as the legitimate rulers of the country following the deposition of James VII of Scotland and II of England in the so-called Glorious Revolution of 1689. The Anglican (Episcopalian) Church in Scotland continued to give their allegiance to James and his Stuart successors, thereby consigning themselves, along with their fellow Jacobites in the Roman Catholic Church, to official opprobrium and persecution for much of the eighteenth century.

Three queens who between them reigned for 179 years have made a particularly notable contribution to the nation's spiritual life and Christian character. Elizabeth I, who ruled from 1558 to 1603, steadied the ecclesiastical ship which had veered so violently from one extreme to another under her predecessors, Edward VI and Mary Tudor, and established a broad and settled Church of England with the monarch as its Supreme Governor. She also personally exemplified the moderate and eirenic theological approach shown by Anglicanism at its best in her statement that 'I have no desire to make windows into men's souls' and in the answer she gave when questioned about her own opinion of Christ's presence in the sacrament of communion:

> *'Twas God the word that spake it,*
> *He took the Bread and brake it;*
> *And what the word did make it;*
> *That I believe, and take it.*

These words have been quoted in the context of recent controversies both within and between different Christian denominations about the precise meaning of the Eucharist by several of those seeking a common ground on the basis of what has been well described as the Queen's 'mystical ambiguity'.

Victoria, whose reign stretched from 1837 to 1901, had a deep Christian faith which she was not shy of sharing with her subjects. Indeed, her frequent visits to those living in cottages around the estates at Balmoral and Windsor often took on the character of evangelistic encounters. On one such visit, she took the wasted hand of a woman who had been ill, telling her, 'I come not as a Queen, but as a Christian lady' and said, 'Put your trust in Jesus, and you will soon be in a land where there is no pain. You are a widow, so am I; we shall soon meet our beloved ones'. On another occasion, when asked by the Queen what she could do for her, a 'lonely cottager' said she would be very glad if 'Your Majesty would just promise to meet me in Heaven'. Softly and firmly came the Queen's reply: 'I shall do so in virtue of the blood of the Lord Jesus Christ'.[7] Arising from her attachment to the simple worship that she experienced at Crathie Kirk while staying at Balmoral, her personal intervention played a decisive role in preventing the disestablishment of the Church of Scotland despite it being the policy of successive Liberal governments. Indeed, her refusal to sanction the Queen's Speech in 1894 if it included such a commitment was the last significant use of the royal veto.

Elizabeth II displayed a similarly deep and committed personal Christian faith throughout the 70 years she ruled between 1952 and 2022, although, unlike Victoria, she did not attempt to intervene politically or constitutionally in the interests of one particular denomination. Rather she showed an equally strong attachment to and interest in both the two churches with which the monarch has a close relationship, the Church of England and the Church of Scotland, while at the same time reaching out more than any other previous monarch to other Christian churches and indeed to other faith groups. Her devoted and sacrificial service, together with her manifest faith, humility and discipleship, led to calls from several quarters after her death for consideration to be given to her canonisation. These came predominantly, though not exclusively, from Roman Catholics who pointed out that she clearly possessed the first of the two formal qualifications for sainthood, 'heroic virtue'. A letter in *The Tablet* advocated taking 'whatever steps may be necessary to put Queen Elizabeth II on the path to sainthood', while the Catholic columnist Charles Moore suggested in the *Spectator* that there would be no difficulty in finding miracles associated with her, in life and death, and looked forward to the speedy canonization of 'St Elizabeth, with Windsor as her Compostela'.[8]

It is highly unlikely that Elizabeth II will be canonized, both because of her own very determinedly Protestant status as Supreme Governor of the Church of England and also, as Charles Moore observed, because she herself would have been 'the person in all the world least likely to have approved of such a proceeding' (although as he rightly went on to say, 'the sort of person who wants to be a saint is the sort who must not be made one'). If she were, however, she would join a small but noble company of sainted and saintly kings and queens. At least two monarchs have been officially canonised – Edward the Confessor in 1161 and Margaret of Scotland in 1250 – and two officially recognised as martyrs – the Anglo-Saxon king Edward, who ruled from 962 to 979, and Edmund, king of East Anglia from 841 to 869. Several others have received unofficial recognition for their sanctity. Both Oswald and his cousin Oswy, who between them ruled Northumbria from 633 to 651, were venerated as saints soon after their deaths. Charles I is regarded as a martyr by many Anglicans and commemorated as such in several church dedications and in services on 30 January, the anniversary of his execution. King David I of Scotland, who earned the sobriquet of 'the Saint' from the number of his religious foundations, is commemorated in the Church of England's Calendar as a confessor. It would be highly appropriate for Elizabeth II to be remembered alongside these predecessors in the Anglican Calendar, perhaps on 2 June, the anniversary of her coronation.

Elizabeth I, Victoria and Elizabeth II shared a broad, eirenic Christian faith and a communal, consensual 'one nation' approach which eschewed fundamentalism and extremism in both theology and politics. All three achieved their considerable spiritual aura and influence partly on the basis of their femininity. Elizabeth I, lauded by poets and courtiers as 'the Virgin Queen', became in the eyes of many a kind of Protestant substitute for the Virgin Mary. Victoria and Elizabeth II in their different ways were revered and loved as mothers and later grandmothers to the nation. Frank Prochaska has argued persuasively that their long reigns saw the feminisation of the British monarchy and a transformation of the institution away from political power and influence to philanthropy and charitable work. The creation of this modern 'welfare monarchy' also owed much to the contribution of other female members of the royal family, notably Queen Alexandra, Queen Mary and Diana, Princess of Wales.[9]

Queens and princesses more than kings and princes attract the kind of veneration which can tip over into monarcholatry, sometimes described as the besetting sin and heresy of the British and a condition that I need to be careful not to succumb to in this book. We have lived so long under a queen that it will take some time to adjust to male rule which is likely to continue for the remainder of this century and beyond. Sacred kingship has its own particular resonances, which will be explored in this book, not least in terms of its expression in contemporary culture and in the Jungian psychological exploration of the male psyche in terms of 'The King Within'. It may indeed be that notions of sacred kingship have a helpful role to play in one of the major social issues of our time, the alienation, under-achievement and low esteem of young males.

This is just one of the ways in which an institution which at first sight seems archaic and even anachronistic may, in fact, have a distinct relevance and purpose today. The medieval accoutrements of the coronation service, the bracelets, armlets and spurs, can powerfully symbolise values of mercy, justice and truth in our jaded and cynical post-modern Instagram age where the visual and the emotional has so much more instant appeal than the rational and intellectual. In a similar way the seemingly counter-cultural values of sacred and Christian monarchy speak to and even perhaps release that latent if largely neglected vein of spiritual and religious awareness in a nation that has stopped going to church and believing in creeds but which has not lost its sense of the infinite and the transcendent and its appreciation of the key Christian characteristics of grace, order, sacrifice and forgiveness.

PART 1
Sacred Kingship in Myth and Scripture

The ideal and the practice of sacred kingship stretch back into the mists of time. The first part of this book explores sacred kingship as an archetype both in primal society and religion and in contemporary popular culture and its centrality in both the Old and New Testaments of the Bible.

Chapter 1

SACRED KINGSHIP

The idea that kings have a spiritual aura and a sacred function is common to virtually all primitive societies. James Frazer, the pioneer anthropologist, began his classic study of magic and religion, *The Golden Bough*, with a lengthy analysis of this subject, noting that:

> … kings were revered, in many cases not just as priests, that is as intercessors between man and god, but as themselves gods, able to bestow upon their subjects and worshippers those blessings which are commonly supposed to be beyond the reach of mortals, and are sought, if at all, only by prayer and sacrifice offered to superhuman and invisible beings.[1]

Frazer saw the origin of sacred kingship lying in the importance of magic in primitive societies and the emergence of particular individuals who were seen to possess supernatural powers.

> The king is the lineal successor of the old magician or medicine-man. When once a special class of sorcerers has been segregated from the community and entrusted by it with the discharge of duties on which the public safety and welfare are believed to depend, these men gradually rise to wealth and power, till their leaders blossom out into sacred kings.[2]

Perhaps the term shaman best describes the figure in primitive societies whose role lies at the root of sacred kingship. Associated particularly with hunter-gatherer tribes in the Arctic regions, but also found elsewhere, shamans were not just involved in conjuring tricks like shape-shifting but acted as seers and prophets and were widely revered for their qualities of discernment and their closeness to the supernatural world. There was a sacrificial element to shamanic power which was exercised on the principle of the wounded healer and through self-giving. The secrets of shamanic union with the other world were passed down from generation to generation, producing a caste which combined the attributes of warrior, philosopher, healer and priest.

The earliest monarchs were almost certainly chosen from these shamanistic families and functioned very much as priest-kings who came to power through a combination of election and hereditary descent. The crowns that they wore may have been based on the shaman's head-dress which itself probably derived from the torque or noose worn round the neck to symbolise the sacrificial posture. It has striking parallels with the Christian image of the crown of thorns as a symbol of suffering and sacrifice which yet also signifies royalty and divinity.

Central to primal notions of the sacred character of kingship was the understanding of the king as the one who took on the forces of chaos, often represented by dragons and monsters, and embodied the principle of order in both the cosmic and everyday world. In mythology the king was located at the *axis mundi,* or centre of the world, a place often associated with a sacred tree, from which he ruled both the natural and social order. He was seen as the steward of the gods, with whom he stood in a special relationship, maintaining the sacred harmonic balance variously described in different religious traditions as *karma, ma'at, dharma, tao* or *torah*.

These aspects of sacred monarchy were clearly apparent in early Celtic societies where the king was seen as possessing special powers of healing and divination and as upholding the moral and spiritual order of his people. In Ireland, the *rí* or *righ* (equivalent to the Latin *rex*, Indic *raj* and Gallic *roi*) held his *fír*, or truth, a mystical entity from which radiated harmony and good fortune. A rule characterised by *firinne flatha* - truth of a sovereign – brought fertility to the land and prosperity to the people, while its opposite, *go flatha* - falsehood of a sovereign - brought about natural disasters. If the king pronounced an untruth, the centre literally ceased to hold and there would be physical as well as moral collapse. A sixth-century legend about the kings of Connaught describes the wall of the royal palace at Tara starting to collapse when the usurper Lughaidh mac Con gave a false judgement. When the true king Corma mac Airt gave a wise and true judgement, however, the wall steadied itself of its own accord.

A striking description of the role of the *fír*, or truth, of the king in upholding the whole order of creation is found in *The Testament of Morand*, which probably dates from the late-seventh century and is the oldest treatise on kingship in the Irish language:

> It is through the truth of the ruler that plagues, a great army, or lightenings are averted from people. It is through the truth of the ruler that he judges great kingdoms, great riches. It is through

the truth of the ruler that he consummates peace, ease, joy, repose, comfort. It is through the truth of the ruler that he drives back great armies as far as the borders of their allies. It is through the truth of the ruler that every heir establishes himself in his fair inheritance. It is through the truth of the ruler that the manna of the great acorn-yield of a great wood is tasted. It is through the truth of the ruler that the milk of a great herd of cattle is enriched. It is through the truth of the ruler that there is every abundance of high, lofty grain. It is through the truth of the ruler that greatness of fish swim in the streams. It is through the truth of the ruler that fair offspring are well begotten.[3]

Kingship seems to have survived longer in Ireland than in other Celtic societies like Gaul where by the century or so before Jesus' birth it had been undermined by the power of the nobility. There was a hierarchy of Irish kings with local rulers, each of whom presided over a *tuath* of a few thousand people, owing fealty to superior kings and ultimately, in the later development of the institution of monarchy, to the high king of Ireland ruling from the sacred hill of Tara. Early Irish sacral kingship was in many respects similar to that found in the Ancient Near East. The king was the special intermediary between humans and gods and stood in relation to his kingdom as the gods stood in relation to the cosmos. He had a specific responsibility for the re-creation of the land and this was sometimes expressed in terms of sacrificial ritual. Irish kings developed a particularly close relationship with their priest-advisers, the so-called druids, who took a key role in choosing monarchs and presiding over their inauguration. As druids took over the old shamanistic tasks of prophesying and passing judgements, kings tended rather to practise reserve and cultivate silence, preserving their sacred aura and distance and just occasionally making solemn pronouncements. In keeping with their sacred cosmological role of maintaining order and harmony, their movements were strictly circumscribed.

Rituals surrounding the choosing of Irish kings gave an important role to supernatural forces. Druids sacrificed a white bull as a preliminary to forecasting a new king. One man was required to consume his fill of the meat of the sacrificed animal and to drink soup made from its blood. As he slept after the meal, four druids sang over him a charm of truth, and the identity of the next king was then revealed to him in a vision or dream. Several stories tell of the involvement of animals and birds in the choosing of a king, and another common motif is a sexual union with a goddess representing sovereignty. Legends surrounding the fifth-century king Niall of the Nine Hostages describe how when out hunting he and his four brothers went to a well that was guarded by an ugly hag. His brothers all refused the woman's demand for a kiss and as a result got no water to quench their severe thirst. Niall, however, threw himself on the woman and gave her a kiss, whereupon she changed to the shape of a beautiful maiden, revealed herself to be 'sovereignty' and hailed him as King of Tara. The word used for the inauguration of a king, *feis,* meant 'spending the night' and carried connotations of sexual intercourse with Meadbah, goddess of Tara, who also gave her name to the ritual drink Meduva proferred to a new king at his inauguration.

The archetype of sacred monarchy is celebrated in all the major world faiths. Jewish and Christian ideas are explored in the next two chapters. The ideal of sacred kingship and royal consecration pervades the pages of the *Rig Veda*, the foundational classic of Hindu spirituality. In Buddhism, the legend of the *Cakkavatti* king, or wheel-turning monarch, is held out as an ideal for lay people to follow, just as the Buddha himself is the model for religious ascetics and monks. In the words of Grevel Lindop:

> It shows that power must grow out of goodness. It demonstrates that inner qualities lead to outer success, and that both must be based on Dhamma – on the sacred laws and traditions of the cosmos – and that we must be ready ourselves to ask for advice from the wise. It shows the part played by the lay person in maintaining the order of the world and suggests that neglect of the poorest and weakest may be the crucial oversight which can lead to the destruction of human society.
>
> Above all it shows the monarch as a symbol of qualities to which all may aspire, and as a secular figure who nonetheless makes the spiritual life possible for himself and others. By living the worldly life in accordance with Dhamma, the wheel-turning monarch becomes a guardian of tradition and the cosmic order for the benefit of all.[4]

Kingship is similarly valued as an archetype and ideal by Muslims. The central theme of the *Shahnameh*, or Book of Kings, the national epic of Persia written in the early eleventh century by Firdowsi, who was influenced by both Shi'ite Islam and Zoroastrianism, is the divine sanction of kingship brought about by *Farr-e-Izadi*, a special grace bestowed upon kings by

God. The poet chronicles the early history of Persia through the reigns of fifty kings, drawing on the Sufi notion of *javanmardi*, or spiritual chivalry, a concept which combines courage, magnanimity, gentleness and modesty in the service of God.

Contemporary expressions of the archetype of sacred kingship

All this may seem a world away from our mindset in twenty-first-century Britain. Yet in appealing more to the heart than the head and belonging primarily to the realm of the imagination, sacred monarchy strikes a distinct chord in our postmodern culture where the emotional and experiential are valued as much as the rational, and the importance of symbol, ritual, mystery and magic is being re-discovered and re-affirmed. The celebration of sacred kingship is a significant theme in contemporary popular culture. There is more than a hint of it in the immensely popular *Game of Thrones* series and it is a pre-eminent motif in the trilogy of films based on J. R. R. Tolkein's epic fantasy novel *The Lord of the Rings*. The final film, *The Return of the King*, released in 2003 and the most successful of the three in terms of box office receipts, Academy Awards and critical acclaim, is essentially the story of the restoration to the ravaged lands of Arnor and Gondor of their rightful king, Aragorn, who rules as the first high king of a vast reunited kingdom, banishing evil and chaos and ushering in the reign of honour, stability and peace. Its overriding theme is the beneficent power and influence of true kingship – when Aragorn takes his rightful crown, the broken sword is mended, the dead tree lives again and joy returns to the kingdom.

A similar message is conveyed in the hugely popular stage musical, *The Lion King*, which has been seen by more than 100 million people in 25 countries since it opened on Broadway in 1997. It, too, is essentially both a celebration and affirmation of monarchy. Its three leading characters are the good, wise king Mufasa, the evil usurper, Scar, and the reluctant heir to the throne, Simba, who eventually comes to realise that he must follow his hereditary duty and destiny and assume the crown in order to rescue the land from famine and anarchy. The musical underlines the themes of cosmic order and sacrifice so fundamental to primal notions of sacred kingship. As Mufasa tells Simba, 'Life rises from death. Everything is connected in the great circle of life. As a king you must understand it.' There is also a strong emphasis on the continuity and tradition of hereditary monarchy. Mufasa also tells his son, 'Look at the stars. The great kings of the past look down to us from those stars. So whenever you feel alone, just remember that those kings will always be there to guide you.' It is when Simba sees the reflection of his dead father's face in a pool that he realizes his own destiny and responsibility.

There has also been an interesting appropriation of monarchy, and more specifically of kingship, as an archetype by psychologists and psychotherapists drawing on the ideas of Carl Jung. In the words of Kathleen Raine, 'it is not the prerogative of any individual, monarch or commoner, but a universal human attribute, of which the monarch stands as a unifying symbol in relation to a particular nation. So understood, kingship is manhood in its fullest development, and queenship womanhood in its fullest development'.[5] This builds on a long tradition of poets identifying kingship with particular qualities and virtues. Shakespeare wrote in *Macbeth* (Act 4, scene 3) of 'the king-bearing graces':

> *As justice, verity, temperance, stableness,*
> *Bounty, perseverance, mercy, lowliness,*
> *Devotion, patience, courage, fortitude.*

What is particularly striking is the recent emergence of a literature which seeks to address the contemporary crisis of male identity by appealing to the model of the sacred king. In Jungian terms, it identifies the archetypes of the masculine psyche as being those of king, warrior, magician and lover, with the king combining and embracing the others. The king archetype stands for promoting order, caring for others and taking personal responsibility. It also has its darker, negative shadows in the tyrant, the usurper and the abdicating king who refuses to acknowledge and take on his responsibilities. This last type, epitomised in *The Lion King* by Simba before he sees his father's reflection in the pool, is taken to represent where many men are. They need to connect with the king archetype and access the king within them. Several psychotherapists present kingship, with its primal associations with order as well as with the sacred, as a ruling and restraining element which needs to be affirmed within the male psyche:

> In terms of a psychic geography, there is no world without the King. Wherever he is, he makes the world, and the *axis mundi*. He is our means for travelling into the sacred dimension. Without the King, the Warrior within becomes

a mercenary, fighting for pay and not for any worthwhile goal. Our Magician becomes a sophist without a King to serve, able to argue any idea convincingly, and believing in none. The Lover without a King becomes a promiscuous philanderer.[6]

In this understanding, accessing the king within is about finding your identity and facing up to your responsibilities. There is a parallel movement to affirm the queen as an image and archetype for feminine maturity and generativity. Although the emphasis in both movements is on accessing an archetype within the individual psyche, they also have a more objective side. One of the main handbooks of the 'King Within' school advises men to contemplate and absorb the attributes of actual kings both in history and fiction. It also makes much of kingly role models drawn from the Christian tradition:

What is truly amazing of course is what we can do, once we access and utilize our King energy. The spiritual systems of the world are designed to bring their worshippers in touch with this empowering energy, whether their leaders know it nor not, because the energy has such a virtuous effect on those who access it. The King's virtue is empowering. Hence Jesus of Nazareth, at least in part, makes an excellent paradigm of the King energy in the individuating male psyche. Hence also the enduring appeal of Ignatius Loyola's exercises. They provide their practitioners with one kind of initiation into the mysteries of the King.[7]

Sociologists, educationalists and criminologists are agreed in identifying a crisis of male identity as one of the most disturbing features of contemporary society, manifesting itself especially in terms of alienation, low self-esteem and poor attainment on the part of young white males. Might further popular promotion of the kingship archetype help to provide a role model and template for male identity? To some extent this has perhaps already been subconsciously and unintentionally done through the work of the Prince's Trust which has helped many young people, male and female, to get out of a rut and fulfil their dreams and potential. Perhaps Charles III, who set up the Trust while Prince of Wales, can carve out a therapeutic and helpful role in society by embodying and promoting this kingship archetype.

Chapter 2

KINGSHIP IN THE OLD TESTAMENT

The origins of Israelite monarchy

The theme of monarchy looms large in the collection of books making up the Hebrew Bible which tells of God's dealing with the chosen people of Israel and forms the Christian Old Testament. The word 'king' occurs 565 times and 'kingdom' 163 times. Six of the so-called historical books have the monarchy as their main subject matter, including the aptly named first and second books of Kings. The life of one particular king, David, occupies more space than that of any other figure, including the great patriarchs, Abraham and Moses.

This is not mere ancient history. Much of the ceremonial and ritual that still surrounds the British monarchy is based on practices described in the Old Testament. This is particularly true of the central sacred act in the coronation service, the anointing of the new monarch with holy oil, which is directly based on the anointing of the earliest Israelite kings as described in the first book of Samuel and the first Book of Kings.

More broadly, the Old Testament provides one of the main sources for our understanding of monarchy as having an essentially sacred character. There are those who regard British monarchs as standing in direct descent from King David and having a special covenant relationship with God as rulers of his chosen people. One does not have to be a British Israelite, however, to sense even in our secularised and de-ritualised age the continuing legacy of Old Testament ideas of kingship. It is there on the face of every coin in our pockets with their abbreviated reminder that the King reigns by the grace of God.

There are early indicators of the value of monarchy in the opening set of books in the Hebrew Bible known as the Pentateuch. The Hebrew word *radah* used in Genesis 1:26 to describe God's intention with regard to the relationship between humans and other living creatures, and usually translated into English as 'dominion', in fact means 'kingly rule' and suggests a gentle, holistic, nurturing and responsible stewardship on behalf of God. Its mistranslation has led to the wholly erroneous assumption that the Bible gives humans a warrant for human exploitation and domination of the rest of creation.[1]

A passage in the Book of Deuteronomy (17:14–20) known as 'the law of kingship' presents the establishment of monarchy in the context of the laws delivered by Moses shortly before his death. It highlights the importance of the Torah, the body of written law, in the Israelite understanding of monarchy, emphasising the king's responsibility to govern under what was the supreme authority in the nation's political life, and to 'fear the Lord his God ... that his heart may not be lifted up above his brethren'.

Kingship is presented in the early books of the Old Testament as both the popularly requested and the divinely appointed answer to the anarchy and disorder prevailing under the judges who ruled the people of Israel for the first two hundred and fifty years or so after their arrival in the promised land of Canaan around 1250 BCE. The latter part of the Book of Judges emphasizes the corruption and lawlessness under this form of government. Its concluding verse notes: 'In those days there was no king in Israel: everyone did what was right in his eyes.'

The inauguration of the Israelite monarchy, which took place around 1020 BCE, is described in 1 Samuel, chapters 8 to 12. A crucial role is played by Samuel, who stands between the old and new systems of government. The last of the great judges, he becomes the first king-maker and presides over the coronations of both Saul and David. He is portrayed as prophet, seer and intermediary between Yahweh/God and the people, to whom the elders of Israel come asking for 'a king to govern us like all the nations'. Samuel puts this request to Yahweh who is initially reluctant to accede to it and tells him to spell out to the people the dangers of kingship in terms of the accretion of private wealth and military might leading to the impoverishment and oppression of the nation. These warnings are ignored, however, and the people continue to insist that they must have a king 'to govern us and go out before us and fight our battles'. When Samuel reports this to God, he is told, 'Hearken to their voice and make them a king.'

In this account of the origin of monarchy, the initiative seems to lie with the people and to be inspired by a desire to keep up with the Canaanites, Moabites and other peoples of the ancient Near East who seem to have been ruled by kings from as early as the third millennium BCE. Yet as the story of the establishment of Israel's monarchy progresses, the initiative shifts to lie with God. Subsequent accounts of the choosing first of Saul and then of David as kings of Israel put the emphasis firmly on their divine election. There is, indeed, a sense of partnership between Yahweh and the chosen people of Israel in the making of kings. Coronations involve the active participation of priests, prophets and elders as well as acclamation by the people. They are also always described as being carried out 'before the Lord'. The impression given here as elsewhere in the Old Testament is of a three way covenant between God, king and people. This concept of covenant is one of the most distinctive and central features of Israelite kingship.

The establishment of monarchy brought the Israelites in line with other tribes of the ancient Near East and they shared the view of kingship common throughout the region, as summarised by Henri Frankfort:

> The ancient Near East considered kingship the very basis of civilisation. Only savages could live without a king. Security, peace and justice could not prevail without a ruler to champion them.
>
> Whatever was significant was imbedded in the life of the cosmos, and it was precisely the king's function to maintain the harmony of that integration.
>
> For the truth about their king affected their lives in every, even the most personal aspect, since, through the king, the harmony between human existence and supernatural order was maintained.[2]

Three features characterised kingship as it was understood in the ancient Near East, and, indeed, throughout the ancient world. First, it belonged primarily to heaven. Those who ruled on earth did so as mediators of divine rule. Second, as part of their role as mediators of divine order in the perpetual struggle with the forces of chaos, human monarchs had a particular responsibility towards the weak, the widows and the fatherless. Third, the sacral nature of kingship and its derivation from heaven was celebrated in annual enthronement ceremonies in which monarchs were renewed in office. These ceremonies often involved a ritual humiliation and reinstatement, linked to fertility rites and the renewal of the cosmic order.

Elements from these three strands found their way into the Israelites' view of kingship. Like their neighbours, they came to endow kings with an almost corporate personality and to see them as the embodiment of their people. The nation as a whole found its focus in the royal house and the personality of the reigning monarch. This meant that the nation's well-being was intimately bound up with the character of the king. The king was seen as the guarantor under God of order, not just in respect of the rule of justice and law, but in more cosmic terms as the one who promoted harmony and dispensed wisdom. Human and mortal though he was, his earthly reign in some sense mirrored and pointed to the divine reign. In the idealised language often used about kingship, he symbolised and exercised through his rule God's attributes of mercy, justice, faithfulness and righteousness.

In his study of the roots of political theology, *The Desire of the Nations,* Oliver O'Donovan identifies three further and more specific functions fulfilled by the Israelite monarchs as God's representatives.

First, they exercised military leadership, undertaking warfare as an almost sacral performance initiated by Yahweh, in Israelite understanding it being God who won military victories and granted them as a favour to the king. Second, they exercised a judicial function, appointing judges and establishing a uniform system of justice to replace competing tribal jurisdictions and clearly standing as the unique mediators of Yahweh's judgements and upholders of the Torah. Third, and most importantly, the Israelite monarchy offered 'the function of continuity, ensuring an unbroken tradition in the occupation of the territory and the perpetuation of the national identity'.[3] These three functions are echoed in the roles of the United Kingdom sovereign today as Commander in Chief of the armed forces, fount of justice in whose name law and order is maintained and to whom judges and magistrates swear allegiance, and symbol of continuity and national unity.

In one crucial respect, the kings of Israel were in a different position from their neighbours. In much of the ancient Near East, as in other primitive societies, the king was seen in some senses as a divine figure, closely related to the gods if not in fact fully of their number. The Israelites had a different understanding of the relationship between monarchy and divinity. Their radical monotheism which clearly separated Yahweh from all creatures did not allow for divine kings. Rulers remained essentially human figures although they were seen to have a unique relationship with and calling from God which was expressed in the descriptions 'son of God' and 'anointed one' which were applied exclusively to kings.

The description of the monarch as son of God occurs, among other places, in several of the Psalms. It is widely thought that this phrase was adopted from near eastern neighbours, and perhaps specifically from Canaanite religion. For the Israelites, however, it did not imply that the king was a divine being but rather that he became God's son by adoption. His sonship was effective not from the day of his birth but from the day of his anointing. References to the Israelite king as the anointed one are also found in a number of Psalms. The anointing of monarchs was widespread in the ancient Near East, being practised by the Syrians as early as the third millennium BCE and also by the Hittites, Egyptians and Canaanites. The Israelites took it over and integrated it into their distinctive understanding of Yahweh's overarching sovereignty and kingship. Indeed, anointing reinforced the sense that the initiative in making kings lay with God, as expressed in Psalm 89:

> *I have found David, my servant;*
> *With my holy oil I have anointed him;*
> *So that my hand shall ever abide with him,*
> *My arm also shall strengthen him.*

The act of anointing, which was usually carried out by a priest, signified the setting apart of the king and signalled his divine election. It was also the moment at which God adopted the monarch as his son and at which God's spirit descended on him. As an act of consecration and setting aside, the anointing of kings was in many ways comparable to the ordination of high priests. There are other striking similarities between kings and priests as they are described in the Hebrew Bible. They seem to have worn the same garments. The word *nezer* is used to describe a form of headgear worn by both high priests and kings. When

David brings the Ark of the Covenant into Jerusalem he is described as 'girded with a linen ephod', a special loincloth which was a specifically priestly garment.

The extent to which Israelite kings exercised a priestly role is difficult to determine. There is one specific if mysterious order of priesthood mentioned in the Old Testament which seems to belong specially if not exclusively to kings. It apparently originated with Melchizedek, a pre-Israelite Jebusite priest-king of Jerusalem who is described in Genesis 14 bringing gifts of bread and wine to Abraham, and it appears to be applied to the Davidic monarchy in Psalm 110, which is often associated with coronations. There are references in the Old Testament to kings offering sacrifices and blessing people in the sanctuary, both acts reserved to priests, but it is not clear whether these were regarded as normal or exceptional activities. The general view of Old Testament scholars is that while kings assumed a supervisory and initiatory role in temple worship, acting almost as 'supreme governors' of the cult, they did not involve themselves in the daily rituals of sacrifices and offerings.

Israelite kings undoubtedly exuded a sacred aura. This was seen as deriving entirely from the fact of their having been chosen and set apart by God. The divine glory and sovereignty were not compromised or diminished by the majesty of the king. Rather the latter was a reflection of and pointer to the former. The monarch's dependence on God is a key theme of Old Testament theology. The king did not stand over or above the covenant that Yahweh made with the people of Israel. Like his subjects he was expected to obey the law and to be totally loyal to Yahweh. Indeed, he was expected to lead the people in loyalty to Yahweh. The prime responsibility of kings was not to win battles, provide economic stability or even maintain justice and peace. Rather it was spiritual – to maintain and oversee the covenant with Yahweh through worship, faithful obedience and trust in the Lord.

Israel's first three kings: Saul, David and Solomon

The man chosen by Samuel to be Israel's first king did not get the institution of monarchy off to a very promising start. Saul is first introduced in terms of his good looks and manly physique, 'a handsome young man' (1 Samuel 9:2) who is taller than any other Israelite. He is pointed out by God to Samuel as the one who will be 'prince over my people Israel. He shall save my people from the hands of the Philistines' (9:16). The context for the establishment of monarchy was one of national emergency when the Israelites were facing the threat of invasion from their oldest and fiercest enemies. While Saul is portrayed first and foremost as a military leader, leading successful campaigns against the Philistines and the Amalekites, his kingship is also represented in more spiritual terms. After being anointed, and 'the spirit of God having come mightily upon him', he meets up with a band of prophets among whom he prophesies, giving rise to the much asked question, 'Is Saul among the prophets?' (10:12). He is, in fact, the only one of the Israelite kings who is specifically portrayed as engaging in prophecy and taking on the mantle of prophet as a function of his kingship.

A careful balance is kept in the story of Saul's elevation to the kingship between the themes of election by God and popular acclamation. There is no doubt that the initiative throughout lies with God who, through Samuel, chooses Saul and causes the divine spirit to descend on him through anointing. Saul is presented by Samuel to all the tribes of Israel at Mizpah as the one chosen by the Lord, whereupon all the people spontaneously shout, 'Long live the king', the acclamation that has sounded out at the proclamation and coronation of every British monarch.

Despite this promising start, the subsequent story of Saul's reign focuses largely on his disobedience of and rejection by God. The matters on which he transgresses seem rather technical – offering sacrifices preparatory to his battle with the Philistines in Samuel's absence and so usurping the prophet's function, sparing the king of the Amalakites, and using his enemies' best sheep and oxen for a burnt offering rather than destroying them as the Lord had commanded. They are, however, enough to make God reject Saul as king and regret ever making him ruler of Israel. The message seems to be that Saul has listened to the people rather than to God – he admits to Samuel that he transgressed the commandment of the Lord because he feared the people and obeyed their voice. Samuel obeys God's command and anoints David with oil whereupon the spirit of the Lord departs from Saul and an evil spirit torments him. Saul descends into madness and paranoia, turning to a medium when the Lord fails to answer him either through dreams or prophets, determining to kill David and eventually taking his own life.

The second Israelite king, David, is introduced in a similar way to Saul, as a bold and courageous military man who will deliver Israel from the Philistines. He, too, is picked out by Samuel, acting on the direct instructions of God, and described in striking physical terms – 'he was ruddy, and had beautiful eyes and was handsome'. From the moment of his anointing by Samuel, 'the Spirit of the Lord comes mightily upon him', even though it is some considerable time before he succeeds as king. In this intermediate period, when he is first and foremost a fugitive from Saul, his character is built up in a highly sympathetic way, not least in terms of his capacity to pardon and indeed to soothe the man determined to kill him. This, almost as much as his military prowess, seems to confirm his fitness for royal office. We are introduced here to a new more gentle paradigm of kingship in terms of healing and forgiveness.

David's kingship, like Saul's, is presented as a matter of popular choice as well as divine election. The tribes of Israel come to him at Hebron, hailing him as the deliverer of the nation and repeating words said to him by God: 'You shall be shepherd of my people Israel, and you shall be prince over Israel' (2 Samuel 5:1-2). This image of the king as shepherd has already featured in David's story. When Samuel first goes to Bethlehem to identify the king that the Lord told him he would find there among Jesse's sons, David, as the youngest, is away looking after the sheep. He would have been overlooked had not Samuel insisted on him being brought in and had the Lord not told Samuel that David was indeed the one to be anointed. For Christians there is a pre-echo here of Jesus the Good Shepherd, but even without this connection the image of monarchs as shepherds exercising pastoral care over their flocks has a powerful resonance. It was picked up in several sermons preached in the days following the death of Queen Elizabeth II.

Forty chapters of the Hebrew Bible are devoted to David's forty-year rule, which probably began around 1000 BCE. By contrast, the four hundred years after his death occupy just 46 chapters. As presented in the Old Testament, his reign marks a significant turning point in the history of Israel from an epic tale of patriarchs, wandering tribes and wilderness to a more domestic and settled story centred on the royal dynasty established on the throne in Jerusalem.

David is portrayed in several different lights – as the heroic military commander and fighting man who sees off the Philistines, Moabites and Syrians; in the gentler guise of the musician who soothes Saul's madness by playing the lyre and the poet who composes psalms; and as the religious leader who calls his people to prayer, initiates and presides over cultic worship, gives the sacred Ark of the Covenant a permanent and fixed dwelling place and personally plans and designs the first temple. In his determination to locate the temple, in Israelite understanding God's resting place on earth, at the heart of his own capital, Jerusalem, we see an early expression of close relations between church and state with the monarchy acting to bring the two together.

David is also portrayed as a man of piety and prayer who takes on an almost priestly role. Several prayers are put on to his lips, including the affirmation recorded in 1 Chronicles 29:10-19 which has been taken up in a number of eucharistic liturgies: 'Thine Lord, is the greatness, and the power, and the glory, and the victory, and the majesty; for all that is in the heavens and in the earth is thine'. He is also credited with being the author of another much-used eucharistic sentence: 'All things come from thee, and of thy own have we given thee.' He is, indeed, the first in a long line of praying kings, a species particularly found in the two books of Chronicles where it is kings rather than prophets who pray.

Although clearly identified as the man who puts kingship on a firm footing after its rocky start with Saul, David is not without faults. He is revealed to be both an adulterer and a murderer. When his mistress, Bathsheba, becomes pregnant, he orders her husband, Uriah, who is one of his own soldiers, to the front line and makes sure that he is killed. David then marries Bathsheba. The prophet Nathan denounces the king's sin and David genuinely repents, leading God to forgive him. This image of the king as penitent sinner is important in showing that monarchs can have their own serious moral failings like other humans, and that for them as for others sincere repentance brings God's forgiveness.

At the heart of David's kingship is the covenant in which God promises its continuance through direct line of succession and the establishment of the dynasty that will bear his name. Unlike his predecessors, Israel's third king, Solomon, comes to the throne not because he is recognised and anointed by a prophet but because he is David's son. The account of his reign is introduced with the story of a dream in which God asks what he would like to be given. Solomon requests wisdom and discernment. Because he has answered in this way and not asked for possessions, wealth, honour, or the life of his enemies, God tells him that he will have all these things as well, 'such as none of the kings had who were before you, and none after you shall have the like' (2 Chronicles 1:12). So begins the most splendid reign of any Israelite king. In respect of his power and prestige Solomon is described as being even more favoured by God than David – 'the Lord gave Solomon great repute in the sight of all Israel, and bestowed upon him such royal majesty as had not been on any king before him in Israel'. Indeed, he comes to be the very epitome of majesty, arrayed in all his glory with the full panoply and pomp of court ceremonial and wealth almost beyond measure.

Yet if Solomon comes to symbolise royalty in its most glittering and ostentatious aspects, he also conforms to the model developed by his father of the king as a priestly figure and man of prayer. He builds the temple in Jerusalem and so fulfils David's project of giving the Lord a dwelling place on earth. He comes to stand for wisdom and discernment, those qualities which he had originally asked of God. His name, which literally translates from Hebrew as 'his peace', has become a byword for wisdom and sage judgement, inspiring the apocryphal book, *The Wisdom of Solomon*, purportedly written by him but in fact most probably the work of an Alexandrian Jew living in the first century BCE. Addressed to kings, it counsels rulers to love justice and cultivate the sagacity, virtue and wisdom that comes from God and reminds them that 'a wise king is the sheet-anchor of his people'.

Even Solomon, however, is not portrayed as a wholly good king. His initial humility, which leads God to shower blessings on him, gives way to complacency and oppressive rule. His heart is turned by idolatry and he incurs divine displeasure. The rending of his kingdom into two halves is portrayed as a divine retribution for his sins in a way that shows that there is an element of conditionality in God's support for the Davidic monarchy and that kings are not immune from divine judgment and censure.

Most of the subsequent rulers of the two kingdoms which result from the splitting of Israel because of Solomon's idolatry are roundly chastised for doing evil in the sight of the Lord and failing to live up to the standards of David. The northern kingdom of Israel is portrayed as descending into idolatry and Baal worship, largely as a result of the apostasy of its first king, Jeroboam, who worships a golden calf, and it is this that leads directly to its destruction and the exile of its people in 722 BCE. The southern kingdom of Judah fares slightly better. Of its twenty kings, twelve are condemned but eight are commended for doing what was right in the sight of the Lord. Two are singled out for particular commendation. Hezekiah, who ruled from around 716 to 687 BCE, destroys the idols which his father Ahaz had worshipped, and reopens the temple. At a time of national crisis and emergency, he puts his trust in the Lord rather than relying on military alliances or seeking to pay tribute to potential aggressors. Josiah, who ruled Judah from around 640 to 609 BCE, similarly leads the kingdom back to God after the apostasy of his father, Amon, holding a covenant renewal ceremony and instituting a new national celebration of the Passover. Despite their endeavours, however, like its northern neighbour, Judah suffers disaster in 597 BCE with the exile of its people and the destruction of Jerusalem at the hands of the Babylonians, who are portrayed as the instruments of divine vengeance against a nation that has been led by its rulers into apostasy and away from covenant obedience to Yahweh.

The Psalms and the monarch as the anointed one

Nowhere in the Hebrew Bible is the sacred role of the king explored more fully than in the Psalms. Many have apparent royal associations. Of the 150 psalms, 73 in the original Hebrew text, and 84 in the Greek Septuagint have the heading *le dawid* (of David) clearly suggesting a royal link, either with King David directly, his dynasty or the royal office. It is quite possible that David instituted the whole tradition of singing psalms – certainly he set up guilds of singers and musicians - and that he wrote some himself although most are of later provenance. Several, known as the 'royal psalms', appear to have been written to be sung at specific ceremonies associated with the monarchy.

The Psalms idealise sacred kingship. The dominant image they present is of the righteous king who is pleasing to God and brings fertility to his land and people. They pick up many of the themes already noted in the historical books of the Old Testament: the king as God's son, servant, covenant partner and anointed one, representing the land and the people before the Lord and leading the nation's worship. Several present the king in a priestly role, notably Psalm 110 which makes a specific reference to 'the order of Melchizedek'. Enthronement psalms celebrating Yahweh's kingship were sung at annual ceremonies where human kings renewed their power and claim to rule. They point to the participation of kings in the great annual festivals of Israelite religion, notably the autumn festival of the booths, or tabernacles, which seems also to have been an enthronement festival. It has been suggested that during these festivals Israelite monarchs may have gone through a ritual process of humiliation and reinstatement and that this was the context for psalms of lament and desolation like Psalms 18, 22 and 89.

Some Old Testament scholars have gone as far as to suggest that the Israelite king may even have had an atoning role, bearing the sins of his people and suffering in some representative way for them. In this interpretation, Psalm 22, quoted by Jesus on the Cross, is taken to be a royal cultic passion psalm which refers to the ritual humiliation of the king and his representative role to suffer on behalf of a suffering nation. If this is the case, then Israelite kings perhaps to some extent anticipated the suffering servanthood and atoning role associated with Jesus. They prefigured him in another way in being frequently described, not least in the Psalms, as God's son and anointed one (*Messiah* in Hebrew, *Christos* in Greek).

During and after the long period of exile that followed the 'Babylonian captivity' of 597 BCE, Jews pinned their hopes on the future emergence of a king from the house of David. This became an ever stronger theme in the following centuries, as expressed in the so-called *Psalms of Solomon*, thought to have been written between 61 and 57 BCE, which look forward to the coming of a new Messiah, or 'son of David', who will be raised up by God to deliver Jerusalem from where he will reign, restoring and re-uniting Israel and bringing about a new world order of justice and righteousness. In the increasingly apocalyptic literature from this period the restored Davidic kingship is linked to the predestined inauguration of a final age.

Quite apart from this messianic eschatological element that comes in towards the end, there can be no doubting the emphasis throughout the Old Testament on the sacred nature of monarchy. It clearly establishes that the institution derives from God, with whom the human monarch stands in a close and special relationship. Within the pages of the Hebrew scriptures we are given vivid pictures of the wise king, the praying king, the psalm-singing king, the temple-building king and the king who mediates and promotes God's covenant with God's people and the divine attributes of mercy, justice and righteousness.

Chapter 3

KINGSHIP IN THE NEW TESTAMENT

The theme of sacred kingship, so fully explored in the Old Testament, continues to figure prominently in the New Testament, although its central focus is on the kingdom of God, inaugurated and proclaimed by Jesus, with its dethroning of the rich and powerful and exaltation of the humble and meek. All four of the Gospel writers use royal titles and monarchical allusions in their descriptions of Jesus. He is identified as the anointed king, promised in the Psalms, the Messiah or *Christos* in Greek, leading his followers to be known as Christians. From his birth in the house and family of David, and his baptism where he is identified by God as his beloved Son, to his trial and crucifixion for being 'King of the Jews', the royal theme runs as a clear thread through his life and death.

Jesus' kingship in the Nativity stories

The importance of the hereditary principle in determining Jesus' identity as the direct heir of David is underlined in the detailed genealogical tables provided by both Matthew and Luke. They provide the basis for the familiar words of the Angel Gabriel to the shepherds at Bethlehem which are sung every Christmas: 'To you in David's town

this day is born of David's line'. There are several
other allusions to Jesus' royal status in the Nativity
accounts in the Gospels. His Davidic descent forms
an important motif in Luke's account of the Angel of
the Lord's appearance to the shepherds to tell them
of their Saviour's birth. The shepherds are located
very deliberately in Bethlehem, the city of David
who was himself a shepherd before he became a
king. Like David, Jesus is a king who comes from
humble origins, being born among the shepherds of
Bethlehem rather than in Jerusalem.

Luke's account of the shepherds being the first
to honour Jesus is paralleled by Matthew's story
of the *magi* who come from the East to Jerusalem
asking 'Where is he who has been born king of the
Jews? For we have seen his star in the East, and have
come to worship him'. This introduces a phrase to
describe Jesus' royal status which is to feature most
prominently in the passion narratives when it is put
on to the lips of his mockers and accusers. The phrase
'king of the Jews' seems to have been used largely
by non-Jews and perhaps first by Hasmonean high
priests, descended from leaders of the Maccabean
revolt, who established an independent state in
Palestine and called themselves 'kings of the Jews'.
It had clear political connotations, and directly
challenged Herod who saw himself as King of the
Jews, but it almost certainly had other more spiritual
resonances as well.

The three gifts which the *magi,* variously
described as astronomers, magicians or wise men,
bring to the infant Jesus also emphasize his royal
status. Gold symbolises his kingship, frankincense
points to his divine being and fitness to be
worshipped and myrrh with its 'bitter perfume'

prefigures his suffering. There are echoes here of accounts of the Queen of Sheba bearing gifts of gold, spices and precious stones to Solomon and of the hope expressed in Psalm 72, traditionally relating to Solomon but often taken as referring to a future Messiah:

> *May the kings of Tarshish and of the isles render him tribute,*
> *May the kings of Sheba and Seba bring gifts!*
> *May all kings fall down before him, all nations serve him!*

It was in the light of these prophetic passages from the Old Testament that Matthew's *magi* came to be elevated to the rank of kings in popular Christian mythology and iconography. This happened very early in the church's history. Tertullian reported that by the end of the second century 'the East considers the *magi* almost as kings' and this identification was certainly taken for granted in the west by around 500 AD. The sixth-century Armenian Infancy Gospel identified and named three specific kings: Melkon (or Melchior as he came to be known in Europe), king of the Persians; Gaspar, king of the Hindus; and Balthazar, king of the Arabs. It described them arriving from Persia with 12,000 soldiers on horseback. By the eighth century the story of the three kings bringing their gifts to the baby Jesus was well established throughout Europe. In the twelfth century, three embalmed bodies in a perfect state of preservation found buried under a church near Milan were declared to be those of the kings. They were transferred to Cologne Cathedral where they became the object of veneration and pilgrimage.

The fact that Matthew's gift-bearing visitors came almost universally to be seen as kings produced a new paradigm of Christian monarchy and a model of the king as worshipper, leading his people in the adoration of Christ, whose majesty he recognised in a particularly acute way because of his own royal position. In their homage to Jesus, the three kings came to represent the peoples of the world and to show the proper attitude for earthly monarchs to adopt towards their heavenly king. This latter theme is reflected in a little-known event in the British royal calendar, the offering of the king's gifts on the feast of the Epiphany described on pages 209-10.

The Gospel writers are particularly inclined to use royal language about Jesus at significant moments of revelation and identification, as after his baptism by John when the voice of God is heard from heaven saying 'This is my beloved Son, with whom I am well pleased', a phrase which echoes the Lord's words to the king he has set on his holy hill in Psalm 2: 'You are my son, today I have begotten you'. The recognition of Jesus as God's son signalled by these words seems to parallel what was understood as happening at the anointing of Israelite kings, the crucial difference being that in Jesus' case it signified recognition of an existing (indeed, pre-existing) state rather than adoption as the son of God at the moment of anointing. At several subsequent points in his life Jesus is accorded kingly status by those whom he meets and who follow him. Nathanael, spotted by Jesus under a fig tree in Galilee, hails him as 'the King of Israel' (John 1:49). His royal status is especially highlighted in the descriptions of his entry into Jerusalem prior to his passion. Matthew describes the crowd hailing Jesus as 'the Son of

David' as they cast their palms before him, Luke has them chanting 'Blessed is the King who comes in the name of the Lord', and John has them hailing 'the King of Israel'.

The entry into Jerusalem

Jesus' entry into Jerusalem offers important pointers both to popular expectations of his kingship and his own understanding of his royal status. All the actions of the crowd bear witness to his majesty. The spreading of clothes on the road along which he is to pass recalls the behaviour of the Israelites following the anointing of Jehu as king, when 'every man of them took his garment and put it under him on the bare steps, and they blew the trumpet and proclaimed "Jehu is king"' (2 Kings 9:13). The strewing of palm branches has a precedent in the reception of Simon Maccabeus, the conquering hero of the Jews, into Jerusalem 'with praise and palm branches' following one of his military triumphs (1 Maccabees 13:51). These actions, and the shouts of 'Hosanna' and other acclamations clearly suggest that the crowd who gather to welcome Jesus into Jerusalem see him as the Messiah coming in triumph into his royal city from which he will rule in majesty.

Jesus himself, however, displays a very different sense of kingship. This is signalled principally by his choice of an ass on which to make his entry into the city. He deliberately opts for an animal associated with humility, humiliation even, rather than a proud charger or stallion more fitting for a king on a triumphal progress. This may be a conscious echo of the ritual public humiliation of the Israelite king during the annual autumn festival of the booths. As portrayed in the Gospels, Jesus' ride into Jerusalem, far from being a triumphal progress, is a journey towards death, its ambivalence well captured in the couplet in Henry Milman's Palm Sunday hymn, 'Ride on, ride on in majesty! In lowly pomp ride on to die'. It demonstrates his re-definition of kingship. He does not reject the people's hailing of him as a king and their belief that he is the heir of David and the promised Messiah but he does reject their expectation of what such a king will be like. Those who welcome him with palms expect a king who will challenge the power of Rome. Instead they get a king who bursts into tears at the sight of Jerusalem. They expect a powerful military commander: they get a prophet proclaiming the reign of righteousness and peace. They expect a conquering hero full of pomp and show: they get a man of sorrows, acquainted with grief and suffering.

Kenosis and servant kingship

Jesus re-defines kingship in more radical ways. As the Son of God, he divests himself of the accoutrements of his royalty and majesty. His *kenosis*, or self-emptying, explored in Philippians 2:5-8, is well described in several classic hymns. Emily Elliott's 'Thou didst leave thy crown, and thy kingly throne when thou camest to earth for me' goes on to acknowledge Jesus' 'royal degree' and speaks of him regaining his crown in heaven. In similar vein, Caroline Noel's 'At the name of Jesus' speaks of one who is 'humbled for a season' and then raised 'to the throne of Godhead'. It ends with the injunctions 'in your hearts enthrone him', 'crown him as your captain' and 'confess him King of glory now'. A more recent hymn by

Graham Kendrick, 'Meekness and majesty' explores the paradox at the heart of Jesus' kingship. Another of Kendrick's hymns, 'The Servant King', perfectly sums up the life and mission of Jesus as the one who 'entered our world ... not to be served but to serve', echoing words that Jesus uses of himself as the Son of Man, recorded by both Matthew and Mark. In this, and throughout his life and ministry as it is described in the Gospels, Jesus overturns worldly expectations of monarchy and shows himself to be a servant king, perhaps most dramatically by washing the feet of his disciples. This ideal of servant kingship has been at the heart of the model of Christian monarchy. It was lived out in a remarkable way by Queen Elizabeth II, as recognised in the title of a booklet published by the Bible Society to mark her 90th birthday entitled 'The Servant Queen and the King she Serves'. Jesus' action in washing his disciples' feet is the inspiration for an important sacred event in the monarch's calendar, the Royal Maundy Service (pages 211-12).

The Passion and Crucifixion

Jesus' kingship is nowhere made more of by the Gospel writers than in the Passion narratives where the application of royal language reaches its zenith, albeit often employed in a derogatory and mocking way. It is especially evident in the mock coronation by the Roman soldiers who robe him, put a crown of thorns on his head, and according to Matthew's account, also hand him a mock sceptre in the form of a reed. The chief priests also mock him when he is on the cross as 'the Christ, the King of Israel' and he is mocked again as a false Messiah after crying out to God in the opening words of Psalm 22. This psalm, as we have seen, may have been associated with the ritual humiliation of the king acted out at the annual enthronement festival in Israel. Its use in the context of Jesus' crucifixion raises the question of how far the Gospel writers were aware of this connection and sought to portray Jesus as the mocked and rejected king with a redemptive and representative role in bearing and atoning for the sins of his people through his suffering. This theme is also suggested in Jesus' own words that 'the Son of Man must suffer'.

The phrase 'King of the Jews', first used by the *magi*, is taken up by Jesus' accusers and inscribed as a title on his cross. It is widely accepted that Jesus was, indeed, crucified for being, or claiming to be, the King of the Jews, a political offence in the eyes of the Romans because it constituted a challenge to the rule of Herod, the Roman-appointed puppet king, and a religious offence in the eyes of Jews who did not recognise him as the true Messiah and saw him as a false prophet claiming to be the son of God. In all the Gospels Pontius Pilate repeatedly asks Jesus whether he is indeed the King of the Jews and receives the non-committal answer 'You have said so'.

Did Jesus see himself as a king?

Jesus was put to death for being, or claiming to be, the King of the Jews. But what was his own attitude to this title? Did he see himself as a king, and if so, of what kind? Although he never volunteers the title when speaking about himself, he never contradicts it when it is used by others. He does use the term 'Son of Man' of himself. Whether this had messianic and royal connotations is a matter of much debate but it certainly seems to have been associated in inter-testamental times with the person of the Davidic heir, as in the Book of Daniel where the Son of Man is described as having 'sovereignty and glory and kingly power'. Jesus' self-identification as 'the good shepherd' in John 10:14 may also have royal connotations, specifically with Davidic monarchy, which, as we have seen, was particularly associated with shepherd imagery.

Jesus comes closest to defining his own sense of his kingship in his exchange with Pilate, which is recorded in most detail in John's Gospel. In response to Pilate's repeated question as to whether he is King of the Jews, Jesus simply says, 'My kingdom is not of this world.' This statement suggests that his kingship has a more radical quality, either being essentially spiritual and rooted in heaven rather than earth, or counter-cultural and opposed to the values of the world. When Pilate goes on to say 'So you are a king?' Jesus answers, 'You say that I am a king. For this I was born, and for this I have come into the world, to bear witness to the truth'. This statement is as far as he is prepared to go. He makes no answer to Pilate's follow-up question, 'What is the truth?' Are we given here a paradigm of the king as truth-bearer, and specifically as bearing witness to the truth sent from above, somewhat similar to the concept of *fir* in Irish sacred kingship?

The kingship of Jesus and what it says about human monarchy

The kingship of Jesus is complex and ambiguous. It is shot through with the paradox of meekness and majesty, suffering and triumph. It involves both the realisation of the ideals and hopes expressed in the Old Testament and a radical re-definition of what lies at the heart of kingship. Oliver O'Donovan points out that Jesus takes on two distinct monarchic roles:

> There is the mediator of God's rule, the role focussed centrally upon the Davidic monarch ... and there is the representative individual, who in lonely faithfulness carries the tradition of the people, its fate and its promise, in his own destiny.[1]

Jesus is portrayed in the New Testament as the servant-king, the priest-king and the prophet-king who bears witness to the truth. His kingship is expressed in terms of his birth in Bethlehem as the direct heir of David, his recognition as God's beloved son and his popular acclamation as the Messiah, and also through his acts of obedience, humility and suffering. His crown is made of thorns and his throne is the Cross. Yet he is nonetheless a king for all that, both during his earthly life and in his risen and ascended state seated on the right hand of his father in heaven.

The festival of Christ the King, instituted by Pope Pius XI in 1925, is now celebrated by many churches of different denominations on the last Sunday of the Christian year. The collects for this Sunday speak eloquently of Christ's kingship in its different aspects. That for Year A speaks of Jesus' 'sovereignty over every age and nation' and asks God that 'we may be the subjects of his dominion and receive the inheritance of your kingdom'. The Year B prayer asks that 'we may imitate the sacrificial love of Christ our King and, as a royal and priestly people, serve you humbly in our brothers and sisters'. The prayer for Year C points to the Saviour who was rejected and acknowledges that 'the mystery of his kingship illumines our lives'.

How does Christ's kingship relate to the human institution of monarchy? Does it render human kings redundant, or indeed idolatrous? At first sight, this might indeed seem to be the case. Jesus is presented in the New Testament as an all-sufficient Lord and Saviour. If we are to enthrone him in our hearts, can there be room for the claims of any other ruler when, as the Book of Revelation so powerfully insists, there is only one throne and 'sovereignty over all the world has passed to Our Lord and his Christ' (Revelation 11:13)? Has he not completely fulfilled the messianic promise and served as the final priest-king, the last in Melchizedek's line, inaugurating God's kingdom and so bringing all human kingdoms to an end? Are not all his followers in some senses both kings and priests, as suggested by Peter's words to the Gentile Christians scattered throughout Asia Minor in latter half of the first century: 'You are a chosen race, a royal priesthood, a holy nation, God's own people' (1 Peter 2:9)?

There is another respect in which Jesus might seem to have spelled the end for human monarchy. Much of his teaching amounts to a sustained attack on human hierarchies and authorities. The Magnificat sets the tone by casting him as the one who 'has put down the mighty from their seat and has exalted the humble and meek'. Jesus preaches that 'the last shall be first and the first last.' His preference, eloquently stated in the Beatitudes and lived out in practical terms throughout his ministry, is clearly for the poor and the dispossessed rather than the rich and powerful. He is portrayed by both the Gospel writers and Paul as a counter-king to Caesar who was the centre of a considerable cult in the first century Mediterranean world. Yet although he challenges human presuppositions about authority and hierarchy and is clearly deeply uneasy about worldly power and the way it is often exercised, Jesus never explicitly attacks the institution of human kingship. His remark, 'Render to Caesar that which is Caesar's and to God that which belongs to God' (Matthew 22:21) and his question to Peter about from whom the kings of the earth take toll and tribute (Matthew 17:25) rather suggest that he sees human rulers as having a legitimate role and a legitimate claim on the allegiance of their subjects.

There are those who argue, quite understandably, that Jesus' own topsy-turvy kingship and the clear thrust of his teaching leave no room for human monarchies with 'all their boasted pomp and show'. Yet it is also possible to hold that in re-defining but not repudiating the institution, he establishes a model for human monarchy patterned on his own royal attributes of righteousness, justice, mercy, wisdom, peace, humility and sacrificial service. There is, to quote the words of the Book of Common Prayer, a place for 'Christian kings, princes and governors' ruling by these principles, remembering the words of Mark 10:43:'Whosoever will be great among you shall be your minister', and standing as subjects of the kingdom of God, and followers of the risen and ascended Jesus Christ, 'the faithful-witness, the first-born of the dead, and the ruler of the kings on earth' (Revelation 1:5).

PART 2
Christian Monarchy in British History

The next two chapters chart the historical development of Christian monarchy in the British Isles over the last 1500 years, chronicling its evolution from the early Middle Ages through the period of the Reformation and the tumultuous seventeenth century to modern times.

Chapter 4

CHRISTIAN KINGSHIP IN CELTIC, ANGLO-SAXON AND MEDIEVAL BRITAIN

With the coming of Christianity into the British Isles from the fifth century, the sacred nature of monarchy was reinterpreted and reinforced by the incorporation of insights and practices from the Old and New Testaments. Kings were among the first converts to the new religion, being targeted by the early missionaries who realised that in tribal and hierarchical societies the way to reach people was through their rulers. For monarchs, whose subjects often followed them in mass conversions and baptisms, Christianity brought the promise of salvation and a kingdom in heaven as well as on earth, divine protection and the expectation that in war God would give them victory over heathen enemies. The church offered legitimation and rituals of inauguration and blessing as well as providing a new cadre of learned men who could write and record events, flatter their royal patrons and help them to frame laws and promote order and stability. In return, kings provided land, substantial endowments and protection to monasteries and churches.

These mutual benefits to crown and church are well illustrated in the life and deeds of the first English king to convert to Christianity. Aethelbert, who ruled Kent from 587 to 616, seems to have come to faith through a combination of the influence of his wife, Bertha, the daughter of a Frankish Christian king, and the preaching of Augustine, who arrived in Thanet with monks in 597, having been sent from Rome by Pope Gregory. According to one account, 10,000 of Aethelbert's subjects followed him in converting and underwent a mass baptism. Among his first actions as a Christian king were to issue the first set of laws in the English language and to grant land to Augustine on which to build an Abbey in Canterbury, the forerunner of Canterbury Cathedral. Aethelbert supported Augustine's church building and evangelistic work as the first Archbishop of Canterbury and later endowed a second church and bishopric at Rochester. In return, the Pope showered the king with both temporal gifts and spiritual blessings, telling him

> Almighty God raises up certain good men to be rulers over nations in order that he may by their means bestow the gifts of his righteousness upon all those over whom they are set. We realise that this has happened to the English race over whom your majesty is placed, so that, by means of the blessings granted to you, heavenly benefits may also be bestowed upon your subjects.[1]

Columba the king maker

At the other end of the British Isles, an Irish monk who died in the year that Augustine came to Canterbury was equally committed to promoting the new idea of Christian kingship. Columba, best known for founding the monastery on Iona off the west coast of Scotland, was instrumental in forging the close bonds between king and priest, and the broader alliance between crown and church which were to help define the Christian character of monarchy in Britain.

In an age when there was political anarchy and violence as well as spiritual and cultural darkness, Columba looked to the new institution of monarchy to provide order, stability and community in place of the arbitrary rule of warlords and chieftains. He was happy to throw the support of the church behind kings who would exercise power under the law and in accordance with Christian principles of justice, humility and mercy. He also realised the benefits to the church of having royal patronage and protection. His decision to leave his native land and settle in the new Irish colony of Dál Riata in the region now known as Argyll on the west coast of Scotland may have been made in response to a call from its king, Conall mac Congall. Some sources suggest that Columba made Conall's stronghold at Dunadd on the Kintyre peninsula his first port of call after sailing across from Ireland around 563 and that the king subsequently gave him the island of Iona for his monastic foundation. The close relationship forged between Columba and Conall proved mutually beneficial to their successors. It ensured royal patronage and protection for the church centred on Iona while greatly enhancing the prestige and legitimacy of the kings of Dál Riata.

Thanks to Columba, Dál Riata may well have been the first region in mainland Britain to experience Christian kingship, two decades or so before Aethelbert's rule over Kent. It may also conceivably have been the site of the first ever Christian royal inauguration ceremony in Europe (see page 118). Several of the earliest lives of Columba cast him in the role of king-maker. One tells of him promising the kingship to Conall's cousin, Aedán mac Gabhráin, and his descendants on condition that they are loyal to his successors as abbots of Iona. Adomnán's later life devotes a chapter to this episode, describing an angel of the Lord visiting Columba and commanding him to ordain Aedán as king. It also describes a subsequent discussion with Aedán as to who will succeed him. The king mentions his three oldest sons, but Columba prophesies that each of them will be slaughtered in battle and asks Aedán if he has any other younger sons, prophesying that 'the one whom the Lord has chosen will run directly to my arms.' Aedán's younger sons are duly called and one of them, Eochaid Buide, rushes up and leans on Columba's bosom whereupon the saint kisses and blesses him and says: 'This one will survive to be king after you, and his sons will be kings after him.'[2] This story, with its close echoes of the choosing of David to replace Saul, is clearly designed to present Columba in the guise of Samuel as a king-maker under the direction of God.

Oswald

Among those who sought sanctuary on Iona from violence in their own lands was Oswald, an Anglian prince who fled there around the year 616 as a teenager with his brothers after the defeat of their father, who ruled the area that was later to become Northumbria. Oswald became a Christian and was baptized on the island. In 634 he took on the Welsh usurper Cadwollan in an attempt to regain the Northumbrian throne from which his father had been ousted. During the night before the battle he had a vision of Columba who promised him protection and prophesied that Cadwollan and his forces would be routed. Immediately before the battle, Oswald knelt down and prayed before a simple wooden cross. He asked his soldiers to join him and they promised that if they won they would convert to Christianity. Oswald's forces were victorious and the site of the battle was subsequently named Heavenfield and associated with miraculous happenings. Oswald asked the abbot of Iona to send a missionary bishop to establish a church in his extensive new kingdom which stretched from Edinburgh to the Wash. The first monk sent down was too severe and austere to win the Northumbrians over to Christianity but his replacement, Aidan, became a highly effective and much loved evangelist. In 635 he founded a monastery on the island of Lindisfarne, strategically situated near the royal stronghold of Bamburgh but also remote enough to be a place of prayer and retreat.

Oswald, who forged a close relationship with Aidan, is portrayed by the historian Bede as displaying the Christian kingly virtues of charity and piety. On being told as he sat at dinner one Easter Day that there was a crowd of poor people outside asking for alms, he not only gave them food but ordered that his silver dish be broken into pieces for distribution among them, possibly providing the inspiration for the silver coins distributed by later British monarchs on Maundy Thursday. Killed in a battle against the pagan King Penda of Mercia in 642, he was buried at Bardney monastery where a number of well-attested healing miracles took place at his tomb. His right hand, which had distributed food to the poor, apparently remained uncorrupted and was preserved in a silver casket and venerated as a relic at St Peter's Church, Bamburgh, and his skull was later enshrined in the chapel behind the high altar at Durham Cathedral. He stands as the first English monarch who, while not formally canonized, came to take on supernatural powers after his death and was widely revered as a saint.

Arthur

Around the same time that Columba was supporting and establishing Christian kingship in Scotland, stories suggest that a British king called Arthur was defending the Christian peoples of Wales and Southwest England against the pagan Germanic Anglo-Saxon invaders. The Arthur of history is a rather shadowy figure but the Arthur of legend stands as the prototype of the noble Christian king, full of valour, chivalry and honour, a British David to Columba's Celtic Samuel.

The earliest source on Arthur identifies him as the victor of twelve battles against the pagan Saxons in the sixth century. He is portrayed not just as a warrior leader but also as a Christian king and holy man whose faith is as important as his military prowess in securing victory over his enemies. He is described as going into one skirmish carrying the image of the holy and perpetual Virgin Mary and as bearing a cross on his shoulders for three days and nights during another battle.

Welsh medieval sources describe Arthur as the High King of Britain with a substantial base in the South West, a considerable Court and close links with the Welsh saints. They also weave a magic spell around him, suggesting that he had a cloak of invisibility and other supernatural attributes. According to the twelfth-century chronicler Geoffrey of Monmouth, Arthur was born at Tintagel in Cornwall, established his court at Caerleon-on-Usk, achieved victories over the Scots and Picts as well as the Angles and Saxons, ruled from York as well as from the South West, and conquered Ireland and Iceland. Betrayed by treachery, he was mortally wounded while putting down a rebellion and carried off to the Isle of Avalon. The last Celtic king before the Anglo-Saxon takeover of Britain, he vowed to return to rescue his native land from its foreign thraldom. So was born the potent myth of the once and future king with its echoes of the Christian belief in the second coming of Jesus.

Embellished in twelfth-century French romances, the adventures of Arthur and his knights of the round table link Christian kingship to chivalry, the pursuit of high ideals and wholesome, manly adventure. His appeal in royal circles was shown in 1187 when Henry II named his grandson after the Celtic hero in the hope that he would one day rule as King Arthur II. In 1191 the bodies of Arthur and Queen Guinevere were 'discovered' lying in a tomb under the floor of Glastonbury abbey, so establishing that the great Celtic king was buried in English soil and confirming the Somerset town, already associated with Joseph of Arimathea and the coming of Christianity to Britain and now firmly identified as Arthur's Avalon, as a national shrine and the focus of a carefully nurtured myth about the continuity of British Christian kingship.

The Arthurian expert Geoffrey Ashe notes that 'from about 1250 onwards Avalon was the pre-eminent shrine of knighthood, the holy place of the monarchy, and the accredited apostolic fountain-head of the British Church'.[3] In 1278, fresh from a campaign against the Welsh, Edward I visited Glastonbury with the Archbishop of Canterbury. The bones of Arthur and Guinevere were briefly exhibited to public view and then entombed with considerable ceremony in front of the high altar.

Later Anglo-Saxon monarchs

By the middle of the seventh century, most of the Anglo-Saxon kings in England had been converted and in 655 Penda of Mercia, the last great pagan king, was killed in battle by Oswy, brother and successor of Oswald as king of Northumbria. Nine years later, Oswy, concerned about discrepancies over the date when Easter was celebrated in his court, convened the Synod of Whitby to sort out differences between Irish and Roman usages and establish uniformity of worship and ecclesiastical practice throughout his kingdom. In taking this initiative, he was acting very much as the Roman Emperor Constantine had done when he called the Council of Nicaea in 325 and asserting the monarch's role as 'supreme governor' of the church within his realms with a responsibility to arbitrate on doctrinal and procedural disputes.

Several Anglo-Saxon kings established ecclesiastical households, made up of priests attached to the court who moved round with rulers on their travels providing regular worship, spiritual counsel and also increasingly performing more secular administrative tasks as well. Priests came to act as secretaries and regularly took charge of the court archives but their principal role remained that of counsellor and confessor. Favoured chaplains were often promoted to bishoprics.

Ambition and political calculation undoubtedly played a part both in wooing kings to Christianity and persuading churchmen to support the crown. For whatever reasons it was espoused, however, the new faith produced a change in the character of Anglo-Saxon monarchy, making it gentler and more humane.

Alfred

One individual in particular came to epitomise the new ideal of Christian kingship both through his own writings and activities and through the cult that grew up around him. The Saxon king Alfred lived from around 849 to 899. The youngest son of King Ethelwulf of Wessex, he accompanied his father on a pilgrimage to Rome where Pope Leo IV administered the rite of confirmation, an act magnified by Alfred's biographer and chaplain Bishop Asser into a consecration to future kingship. His five older brothers were all killed by invading Danes during their brief reigns and Alfred succeeded to the throne of Wessex around 871 with the threat of annihilation hanging over the kingdom. Thanks partly to his innovative use of naval power, he managed to beat back the Danes. Having secured the safety of his kingdom, he devoted the latter part of his reign to administrative and ecclesiastical reforms and to encouraging learning and faith. He promulgated the first systematic set of laws in England, more comprehensive than those issued by Aethelbert three hundred years earlier, drawing heavily on Old Testament law codes, and seeking to promote the principles of justice and equity. He inaugurated a movement of reform in the church, personally translating Gregory the Great's *Treatise on Pastoral Care* into English and distributing a copy to every bishop in the kingdom. It became one of the key texts for the English church, with its emphasis on the role of the pastor as spiritual doctor and preacher, the importance of a learned clergy and preaching by example as much as by word.

Alfred himself took these ideals to heart. He had a strong sense of reserve and restraint, believing that a king should not make a fuss but suffer in silence, a philosophy summed up in a saying attributed to him: 'Do not tell your grief to a lesser man; tell it to your saddle-bow and ride forth singing'. He was also a man of prayer. Deeply attached to the psalms which he memorised as a child, he was, according to Asser,

> in the invariable habit of listening daily to divine services and Mass, and of participating in certain Psalms and prayers, and in the day-time and night-time offices and, at night-time, of going (without his household knowing) to various churches in order to pray.[4]

Alfred consciously followed the Old Testament model of the king as the leader of his people in worship and promoter of religious revival. He followed its teaching that repentance and reform were as important to national security as a standing army and navy. Believing that England's conquest by the Danes was both a consequence of and a judgement on its apostasy and abandonment of Christian learning, he embarked on a personal crusade to renew religion in his kingdom. Appalled that clergy were largely ignorant of the meaning of the Latin words that they recited daily, he assembled a team of scholars from across the British Isles to work at his court promoting clerical education and translating key Latin texts into English.

It was not surprising that in his biography Asser drew frequent comparisons between Alfred and Solomon. He was also compared to David, who, like him, had been anointed as a child above his brothers and lived as a fugitive in hiding before consolidating his crown through military prowess. The figure depicted in the centre of the Alfred jewel, the small golden pendant apparently made for him, which was found in Somerset in 1689 and is now in the Ashmolean Museum, Oxford, may be that of David, holding in his hands the rod of judgement and staff of comfort mentioned in Psalm 23. Like David, Alfred saw himself as leading his people in worship and standing at the head of the church as well as of law and government. He believed that his own authority came from God who was his lord, and extended over his subjects to whom he was lord. Kingship was a sacred trust instituted by God for the purposes of good and just government and pastoral care of the people.

Athelstan and the religious compact at Eamont Bridge

A key role in both the unifying and Christianising of Britain was played by Alfred's grandson Athelstan, King of Wessex from 924 to 939. At a meeting at Eamont Bridge, near Penrith in Cumbria, in 927, his supremacy was acknowledged by the kings of the Scots, the Welsh, the Strathclyde Britons and the Northumbrians, who also agreed to suppress idolatrous practices in their territories. This gathering, the first occasion when the rulers of the Celtic realms in the British mainland paid homage to an English king, has been taken as marking the establishment of Christianity as the accepted and official religion of Britain. With his supremacy acknowledged from Cornwall to Scotland, Athelstan could reasonably claim to be, as coins issued during his reign proclaimed, '*rex totius Britanniae*'. A passionate collector of religious relics, he took his responsibilities as a Christian ruler seriously, describing himself as 'supervisor of the Christian household' of his extensive realms. Among the laws that he promulgated was one making Sunday trading illegal.

The religious compact at Eamont bridge seems to have been made specifically to counter the reintroduction of pagan practices into parts of Britain taken over by the Vikings. Although they continued to dominate much of northern and Eastern England during the tenth century, the Vikings did not destroy the pattern of Christian kingship established by the Celts and Anglo-Saxons. Indeed, several Viking monarchs became exemplary Christian kings in the Alfredian mould. One such was Canute, whose famous encounter with the waves was, according to one tradition, an exercise in Christian humility in which the king rebuked the flattery of his nobles by demonstrating that not even he could halt the movement of the tide.

By the end of the first millennium the institution of Christian kingship was firmly established throughout the British Isles. Monarchs were the principal patrons and protectors of the church. The great majority of the monasteries and minsters which provided pastoral care and worship before the establishment of parish churches were royal foundations, built on land provided by kings and supported by their endowments. Establishing religious houses was a favourite royal activity, following in the tradition of Alfred who had set up a monastery at Athelney, his base in Somerset, and Athelstan, who founded Malmesbury Abbey where he was subsequently buried. This activity was continued by later Anglo-Norman monarchs and notably in eleventh-century Scotland by Queen Margaret, a deeply pious woman who brought Benedictine monks from Canterbury to staff the church at the royal capital of Dunfermline and supported the ailing religious community on Iona.

Sacred titles taken by medieval kings

Christian kingship brought new titles as well as new responsibilities for Britain's rulers. Perhaps the first to be appropriated was that of ruling through the grace of God, or *Deo Gratia*, the idea that is still expressed on every coin of the realm through the abbreviation DG. The late eighth-century Anglo-Saxon king Offa described himself as 'by the divine controlling grace king of the Mercians'. From the mid-tenth century, several English kings also began styling themselves Christ's Vicar or deputy. Edgar, Alfred's great grandson who ruled from 957 to 975, described himself in this way when founding a new monastery at Winchester in 966. He is pictured in the monastery's charter book flanked by St Peter and the Virgin Mary and offering the new foundation to Christ. Some years later Ethelred II stated that 'the king must be regarded not only as the head of the church but also as a vicar of Christ among Christian folk'.[5]

The Christian king's role as Vicar of Christ was understood at various levels. It was a reminder of the monarch's responsibility to promote the Christian faith and defend its cause, a view which reached its apogee during the Crusades when Richard I led a great army to Palestine to stop the holy places of Christianity falling into Muslim hands. It also affirmed a priestly, quasi-episcopal view of monarchy in the tradition of Melchizedek. There was, too, a political dimension to the title. In claiming that they acted as vicars of Christ, England's Norman kings were directly challenging attempt by the papacy to assert more control over the emerging national churches in Europe. Episcopal investiture was the main battleground over which the competing claims of king and Pope were fought. The Norman kings' practice of directly investing English bishops with ring and crozier as well as nominating and consecrating them under royal writ provoked fierce controversy with Rome. A compromise was reached in the reign of Henry I in 1107 whereby bishops received their ring and staff at their consecration, having already done homage to the king. This was not the end of hostilities between the English crown and Rome, however, and both Henry II and John found themselves excommunicated. In 1213 John was forced to concede defeat and acknowledge the subordination of the English church to the Pope.

Behind this struggle lay the realisation by medieval monarchs that the church was one of the most important institutions in their realm and a desire to ensure that its leaders were also chief ministers of the crown. Not that there was any doubt who was master between archbishop and king, as was shown by the murder of Thomas à Becket in 1170 apparently on the orders of Henry II in one of the most disgraceful episodes in the history of the British monarchy's dealings with the church. The idea that kings were superior to bishops was also asserted at a less brutal and more theological level, with the development of the idea that while both bore the image of Christ, the bishop, in the words of an anonymous twelfth-century, tract 'acts as the antitype of the inferior office and nature, that is, His humanity: the king, as that of the superior office and nature, that is, His divinity'. Indeed, monarchs uniquely imitated Christ in having two natures and being both human and divine:

> The king is a twinned being, human and divine, just like the God-man, although the king is two-natured by grace only and within time, and not by nature and within eternity. The terrestrial king becomes a twin personality through his anointment and consecration.[6]

Miraculous powers

This belief that monarchs, like Christ, had two natures, was reflected in the idea that they also had miraculous powers. Oswald of Northumbria was the first English king to possess apparently miraculous powers after his death. Among subsequent monarchs credited with similar posthumous powers, one of the more intriguing is Edgar's son, Edward the Martyr, who was hacked to death on the orders of his wicked stepmother in 978. His body was removed from its original burial place at Wareham in Dorset in 980 after miracles apparently took place there and re-interred at Shaftesbury Abbey to which pilgrims from all over England came to venerate his shrine. Bones unearthed in an archaeological dig there in 1931 were later offered to both the Anglican and Roman Catholic churches but were declined for reinternment as relics. However, the Russian Orthodox Church in exile accepted them and since 1988 they have been in the possession of a small Orthodox Christian community in Brookwood, Surrey.

Touching for the King's Evil

Perhaps the most striking example of the miraculous associations of medieval sacred kingship was the development of the practice of touching for the king's evil. The disease for which the royal touch was regarded as particularly efficacious, known popularly as scrofula and in medical terminology as tuberculous adenitis, was an inflammation of the lymph nodes which often had the effect of making the victim's face putrid. The first English king who is clearly recorded as touching for scrofula was Henry II, although the practice may have originated with Edward the Confessor, as suggested by Shakespeare in *Macbeth* where Malcolm, fleeing from the hatred of the Scottish tyrant and taking refuge in Edward's court, is impressed both by his healing miracles and his 'heavenly gift for prophecy'.

Specially minted coins, known as 'touch pieces', were hung by the king around the necks of those suffering from scrofula. As well as touching those afflicted by the disease, monarchs also often made the sign of the cross and sometimes washed affected parts with water. A related custom which developed in the later Middle Ages was the distribution of cramp rings, made out of gold and silver coins placed on the altar of the royal chapel by the king in the course of his Good Friday devotions. By virtue of their royal consecration they were held to have the power to restore strength to epileptics and relieve muscular spasms.

The practice of touching for the king's evil did not die out with the Reformation. Although Tudor monarchs were not enthusiastic about the practice, the Stuarts revived it. Charles II touched 23,000 people in the four years following the restoration of the monarchy in 1660 and by the end of his reign was touching 6,000 annually, making him the most prolific miracle-working monarch to occupy the English throne. James II touched 4,422 people between March and December 1685, making the sign of the Cross and using Latin as he did so to the discomfort of his Protestant subjects. The last reigning British monarch to perform the ritual was Queen Anne in April 1714. The Book of Common Prayer included a service for the healing of the sick by the monarch from 1633 to 1715. The Jacobite pretenders kept the practice going and Prince Charles Edward Stuart held a healing ceremony on Edinburgh in 1745. There are even perhaps lingering echoes of it today, as shown by the number of people who stretch out their hands to be shaken by King Charles III, Queen Camilla and the Prince and Princess of Wales in their walkabouts.

The Middle Ages saw the flowering of the cult of Christian monarchy in all its branches – splendid and servant-like, pious and chivalrous, full of knightly virtue, gung-ho triumphalism and supernatural magic. At times it could go over the top, as when Richard II had himself depicted in the Wilton Triptych kneeling before the Virgin and Child in the company of John the Baptist, Edward the Confessor and Edmund the Martyr, an East Anglian king who became the object of a popular cult after his death in 869 at the hands of 'the great heathen army' of the Vikings. Angels look on wearing his badge of the white hart with a golden chain around its neck. Shakespeare was almost certainly aware of this portrayal when he wrote his play *Richard II* which is full of references to sacred kingship and contains the observation that 'Not all the water in the rough rude sea can wash the balm from the anointed King.'

Yet if medieval monarchy developed a magnificence that echoed the splendour of Solomon's court and its more worldly trappings, it also espoused the theme of the servant-king and acknowledged its utter dependence on God's grace. Both these elements were reflected in the civic triumphs staged in the later Middle Ages, often around Epiphany or Advent, for the entrance of monarchs into the cities of their realms with the king being portrayed as the type of Christ with *Majestas Domini* and the queen as the *Virgo Mediatrix* and bearer of heavenly glory. Deliberately modelled on Jesus' entry into Jerusalem, these ceremonial entries of medieval monarchs into their capital cities also often served as a reminder of the journey to be undertaken by all souls, including royal ones, towards death and the throne of heaven.

Chapter 5

CHRISTIAN MONARCHY IN BRITAIN SINCE THE REFORMATION

Since the Reformation Protestantism has been the single most important influence on the sacred nature of the British monarchy. It has led to a continuing emphasis on the biblical roots of kingship, the close involvement of the Crown in church affairs and in such important ventures as the production of the Book of Common Prayer and the Authorised Version of the Bible, and the association of the monarchy with the virtues of duty, philanthropy and public service. The seventeenth-century doctrine of the divine right of kings and the notion of covenanted or limited monarchy that came to replace it were also and equally products of the Reformation.

Monarchy and the English Reformation

The crown played a crucial part in the English Reformation which was initiated by Henry VIII with the help of his loyal lieutenant Thomas Cranmer. Together they created what was effectively a nationalised state church of a moderately Protestant hue with the monarch at its head, bishops and a conservative liturgy in English. Subsequent sovereigns made their influence felt on the emerging

Church of England, with Edward VI steering it in a much more Protestant direction and Elizabeth steadying it to produce the Anglican *via media* which has remained one of its distinguishing characteristics to this day.

Tudor kings and queens pursued an active, 'hands-on' approach in their dealings with the church over which they presided, personally appointing and removing bishops and promoting liturgical reforms. The Royal Injunctions Act of 1536, which required all parish churches to acquire and display a copy of the newly authorised English Bible, reflected Henry VIII's personal commitment to using the vernacular language in worship. His intervention was almost certainly behind the subsequent requirement that all lessons in matins and evensong were to be read in English. Edward VI played a key role in the preparation of the first English Prayer Book of 1549. His boyish enthusiasms (he was only nine when he began his six-year reign) progressed the advance of Protestant practices and the disappearance of Catholic ones in the English church. On a visit to Westminster Abbey shortly after his coronation he ordered that the number of candles used at communion be reduced to two, the ringing of bells be limited to before and after the service and discontinued at the moment of consecration, the choir give up tonsures and the clergy cease wearing monastic habits. The young king took an active lead in promoting the singing of metrical psalms in church services and, more regrettably, signalled his approval for the wave of iconoclasm which destroyed chantries and parish churches. Elizabeth I also took a strong and active interest in church affairs and frequently interrupted preachers if she felt they were wandering off the subject.

Much appeal was made to Old Testament texts and precedents by churchmen preaching and writing about the Tudor monarchy. Edward VI was compared with Josiah, an earlier boy-king who had purged his land of idols and whose discovery of the 'Book of the Law' was taken as a direct precedent for the production of the Prayer Books of 1549 and 1552. In his coronation sermon, Cranmer described Edward as 'a new Josiah' who would put aside idolatry, guard against vice, reward virtue and practise righteousness. Hailed as the Virgin Queen and the bride of the Church, Elizabeth was regularly compared to David in her struggles against the papacy. Preaching before her in 1570, Edward Dering, a Puritan divine, took as his text verses from Psalm 78 referring to the election of David and spelt out his understanding of the monarch's spiritual responsibilities: 'It is true that the prince must defend the fatherless and the widow and relieve the oppressed...But this is also his duty, and his greatest duty: to be careful for religion, to maintain the gospel, to teach the people knowledge and build his whole government with faithfulness.'[1]

In appealing to the model of the Israelite monarchy to support the notion of royal supremacy over the church, Anglican divines were acting very much in the spirit of the wider European Reformation. The idea of the 'godly prince' was a significant theme of Continental Lutheran and Calvinist Reformers alike. The Strasbourg reformer Martin Bucer argued in his *De regno Christi* (1550) that kings rather than bishops would restore the rule of Christ to both churches and nations, while the Swiss reformer, Thomas Erastus, gave his name to the doctrine that the church should be subordinated to and directed by the secular power.

Monarchy and The Scottish Reformation

While England took a broadly Erastian course, the Reformation in Scotland proceeded with quite different consequences for the relationship between church and monarchy. There the impulse for religious reform came from below rather than above and produced a strong Protestant antipathy against hierarchies and authorities. As James VI wistfully remarked in 1600, 'the reformation of religion in Scotland' was wrought 'by a popular tumult and rebellion ... not proceeding from the Princes ordour (sic), as it did in our neighbour country of England'.[2] While there was general enthusiasm among the Scottish reformers for the notion of a godly commonwealth ruled by a godly prince, they were strongly opposed to the monarch being head of the church, a position that was reserved for Jesus alone.

Experience of persecution and exile under the Catholic Mary Queen of Scots led the Scottish reformers to become even less enthusiastic about Crown control over the Church. Their change of view can be clearly seen in the case of John Knox. Initially, he subscribed to the view that subjects owed unstinting obedience to their rulers. In the mid-1550s, as an exile in Geneva, Knox changed his position and argued that subjects had the right to rebel against a tyrannical or ungodly monarch, a theme that he developed most vigorously in his famous *First Blast of the Trumpet Against the Monstrous Regiment of Women* with its vitriolic attack on Mary Tudor. By 1559 he was arguing that in a godly commonwealth both monarch and subjects alike are equally members of the church and subject to its disciplines. This became a key theme of Scottish Presbyterianism much to the annoyance of successive Stuart monarchs not least the first in the line, James VI of Scotland and I of England.

James VI and I

The first sovereign to be crowned in and rule over both England and Scotland took a high view of the sacred dimension of kingship and set out the theory of the divine right of monarchy with which the Stuart dynasty that he inaugurated was to be particularly associated.

He gave a full exposition of it in a two hour lecture to the English Lords and Commons assembled in 1610:

> Kings are not only God's lieutenants upon earth, and sit upon God's throne, but even by God himself they are called Gods ... Kings are justly called Gods, for that they exercise a manner or resemblance of divine power upon earth. For if you will consider the attributes of God, you will see how they agree in the person of a king. God has power to create, or destroy, make, or unmake at his pleasure, to give life, to send death, to judge all, and to be judged nor accountable to none ... And the like power have kings. They make and unmake their subjects; they have power of raising and casting down; of life, and of death. Judges over all their subjects, and in all causes, and yet accountable to none but God only.[3]

James's exalted view of monarchy was accompanied by a strong sense of his religious responsibilities.

Brought up as a devout Presbyterian, he regarded himself as the benevolent 'nursing father' of the Scottish Kirk. The Scottish Reformers for their part also had high expectations of him in this respect. At his Scottish coronation in 1567, the infant king was compared by John Knox to the Israelite king Joash, and when he entered Edinburgh at the age of fourteen he was hailed as another David and as the godly prince of a Protestant people. Initially he gave strong support to the reformed church in Scotland and to its Presbyterian government and structures. All parish ministers were instructed to ensure that their parishioners subscribed to the 'King's Confession', a statement of Protestant principles drawn up by his chaplain. The so-called Golden Act of 1592, which recognised the Presbyterian system of church government, gave the king the right to decide the time and place for future meetings of the Church of Scotland's general assemblies, all of which James attended from 1597 until his departure south to ascend the English throne in 1603.

James found the Anglicanism which he encountered when he became king of England rather more to his royal taste than the Presbyterianism in which he had been reared in Scotland. To the consternation of his erstwhile supporters in the Scottish Kirk, he sought to establish in his northern kingdom the Church of England's episcopal system of governance and doctrine of royal supremacy. Subsequent Stuart monarchs followed suit with disastrous results: Charles I's attempts to impose the English Prayer Book and episcopal system on the Scottish church provoked the so-called 'Bishops' war' in Scotland which in turn led to the English Civil War.

King James Bible

James's most lasting and precious contribution to the religious life of the newly united kingdom of Scotland and England was his patronage of the version of the Bible which bears his name and came to be one of the most significant books in the English language in cultural as well as religious terms. Originally conceived at a meeting of the Church of Scotland General Assembly that he attended in Burntisland Parish Church in Fife in 1601, the new translation was commissioned at a conference called by James at Hampton Court three years later. The king laid down clear instructions for the methodology, staffing and timetable of the project and continued to take a keen interest in it until its completion. He was concerned that the new Bible should not be a narrow reflection of a single theological position. However dogmatic his views on monarchy, in theology he strove for breadth and moderation, maintaining 'I am for the medium in all things'. He deliberately brought together Puritan and High Church translators to collaborate on what he hoped would be an *irenicon*, or instrument of peace and unity founded on his own divine authority. In the words of Adam Nicolson, who has written a superb book on the making of the King James Bible:

> Its subject is majesty, not tyranny, and its political purpose was unifying and enfolding, to elide the kingliness of God with the godliness of kings, to make royal power and divine glory into one indivisible garment which could be wrapped around the nation as a whole. Its grandeur of phrasing and the deep slow music

of its rhythms – far more evident here than in any Bible the sixteenth century had produced – were conscious embodiments of regal glory.[4]

Iconography of sacred monarchy

Alongside their attempts to impose their own religious preferences on their often unwilling subjects, the Stuart monarchs also had a fascination with the romance and tradition of medieval sacred monarchy. Perhaps because they were the first dynasty since the Norman Conquest to be free of competing claims to the throne, being heirs to the houses of Tudor and Plantagenet as well as to all Scottish kings since Robert the Bruce and being responsible for uniting the thrones of Scotland, England and Wales, the Stuarts had a strong quasi-religious sense of their role in renewing and uniting the British people. In taking the oak as the royal symbol they emphasized the regenerative powers of the Crown and appealed to both pre- and post-Christian Celtic notions of sacred kingship. In giving the name Britain to the new united kingdom over which he presided, James VI and I was widely seen as consciously comparing himself to Arthur. The fact that the execution of a Stuart king in 1649 brought about the apparent end of monarchy before its restoration eleven years later further encouraged parallels with the ancient motif of the dying and rising king and indeed with the death and resurrection of Christ.

This conscious cultivation of the sacred dimension of monarchy was accompanied by a fascination with iconography. The Stuarts were keen to be represented in paintings in the guise of Old Testament monarchs or with other symbols of sacred monarchy. James I was depicted as Solomon in Rubens' portrait for the Banqueting Hall in Whitehall. Van Dyck painted Charles I seated on a white horse, representing the Word of God, 'faithful and true' as described in the Book of Revelation 19:11-14.

Church leaders enthusiastically joined in the promotion of the divine and sacred aspects of monarchy. The sermon preached at James I's funeral included a long panegyric describing him as the British Solomon and Archbishop Laud had no qualms about describing Charles I as 'the beauty of holiness'. Poets and playwrights added their eloquent tributes. Shakespeare is thought to have inserted passages about the sacred nature of kingship into his plays to flatter James I, notably in *Richard II*.

Charles the Martyr and comparisons with Christ

Following his execution in 1649, Charles I was widely hailed as a martyr and compared to Christ. For those in the crowd outside the Banqueting Hall who pressed forward to soak their handkerchiefs in royal blood, and many others, he died a martyr to the Christian faith and to the Church of England in particular. The widespread cult which grew up around him in death was given a powerful stimulus by the publication on the day of his burial of the *Eikon Basilike: The Portraiture of His Sacred Majesty in His Solitudes and Sufferings*. The cover of this collection of meditations and prayers depicted Charles kneeling and grasping a crown of thorns, his eyes fixed on a heavenly crown and his earthly crown lying discarded at his feet. In the book his words merge with those of David, providing a manual of prayers enabling people to join the dead king in the community of believers.

Signs and wonders at the time of his funeral were taken as further evidence of his Christ-like qualities. A fall of snow which covered his coffin with a white pall as it was being carried into St George's Chapel, Windsor, was seen as a sign that heaven was declaring his innocence. A teenage girl near Deptford was apparently cured of the king's evil by a handkerchief dipped in his blood. Devotion to Charles, king and martyr, was widespread in the Church of England for the next two hundred years. Until 1859 his martyrdom was commemorated with a special service in the Book of Common Prayer on 30 January and services honouring Charles the Martyr are still regularly held on that day.

Comparisons with Christ were regularly made about seventeenth-century monarchs. The medieval notion of the king's two bodies or natures was revived and often explicitly linked to the Christian understanding of the two natures of Christ. At the time of his English coronation in 1661, Charles II was frequently likened to Christ, a comparison which was encouraged by the story that an especially bright star had shone at his birth as well as by the obvious associations prompted by his restoration or resurrection of the monarchy and established church after the dark days of Puritan rule. A poem applied to him the phrase 'he led captivity captive', first found in Psalm 68 and later used of Jesus by Paul in Ephesians 4:8, and portrayed him as the one who would fulfil the prophecy in Isaiah 11 and inaugurate a new age when the lion would lie down with the lamb.

CHRISTIAN MONARCHY

Divine Right

The understanding of the sacred nature of monarchy was boosted by the theory of divine right. This put forward four propositions: that monarchy is a divinely ordained institution, that hereditary right is indefeasible and the right acquired by birth cannot be forfeited through any circumstance, that kings are accountable to God alone, and therefore 'a mixed or limited monarchy is a contradiction in terms', and that non- resistance and passive obedience are enjoined by God. While its origins go back to medieval notions of the king being God's Vicar on earth and reflecting the godhead of Christ where the priest reflected only his manhood, in its full form, divine right was essentially a post-Reformation concept, worked out in opposition to the claims of papal supremacy and closely allied to the development of nation states. In many ways it was a particularly Anglican theory, opposing the clericalism found in both Roman Catholicism and Presbyterianism which sought to limit the sovereign's power over the church.

The two leading seventeenth-century exponents of divine right theory both drew heavily on Old Testament texts. For Robert Filmer, author of *Patriarcha,* kingship belonged to the natural order of society which God had established when he first created Adam, and which embodied the patriarchal system that underlay the life of families and nations. The king ruled as patriarch or father of his people. Thomas Hobbes traced the monarchical system in Israel back to Abraham, whom he saw as the first ruler appointed by God with full rights to legislate in secular and domestic matters. With the election of Saul as king, God ceased to rule his people directly and instead governed through kings who alone had the right to interpret his word. Hobbes further argued that Christ's kingly rule on earth only begins with his second coming. In the meantime it is earthly monarchs who have all power and authority in matters spiritual and temporal.

Covenant theory

The absolutist concept of divine right was not the only theory of monarchy worked out in the seventeenth century on the basis of appeals to the Old Testament. A very much more limited concept of sovereignty was developed by those who took their stand on the covenant theme in Israelite kingship and argued that it was the nation rather than the monarch on which God looked with special favour. This theory was taken up especially in Scotland and was perhaps never better expressed than in the three-hour sermon preached by Robert Douglas, Moderator of the General Assembly of the Church of Scotland, at the Scottish coronation of Charles II at Scone in 1651. He took as his text 2 Kings 11:12-17, which describes the crowning of Joash and the role of the priest Jehoiada in making a double covenant, first 'between the Lord and the king and the people that they would be God's people' and then between the king and his people. Douglas's sermon spelt out a very different doctrine of the monarchy from that held by the proponents of divine right:

> When a king is crowned and received by the people, there is a covenant or mutual contract between him and them, containing conditions mutually to be observed ... It is good for our

king to learn to be wise in time and know that he receiveth this day a power to govern – a power limited by contract; and these conditions he is bound by oath to stand to, for a king's power is not absolute but is power limited by covenant.[5]

This Presbyterian sermon was noticeably free of the adulation and flattery with which most clergymen in the established Church of England addressed the Stuart monarchs. It exhorted Charles to embark on both a personal and family reformation and directed him to seven specific duties – to seek God in frequent and earnest prayer (Douglas having observed that 'prayers are not in much request at Court'); to be careful of the kingdom; to make much use of faithful servants of Christ, whether ministers or laymen; to be careful whom he put in places of trust; to be moderate in his use of authority; to be strenuous against the enemy; and, above all, to be constant. Charles was reminded that there were three categories of monarch in the Old Testament – those who did evil in the sight of the Lord, those who did what was right but not with a perfect heart, and those who did right in the sight of the Lord with a perfect heart. 'Let us neither have the first nor the second but the third written upon our King' preached Douglas, before adding a ringing reminder of the impermanence of earthly kingship:

A king should always bear in mind that even the firmest of earthly crowns is but a fading crown after all: and therefore that he should have an eye upon the 'crown of glory that fadeth not away', and 'the kingdom that cannot be shaken': that crown and kingdom belongeth not to kings as kings, but unto believers: and a believing king hath this comfort that when he hath endured for a while, and been tried, he may receive the crown of life, which the Lord hath promised to them that love Him.[6]

The Glorious Revolution

The dramatic events of 1688-9, when James II was deposed because of his Catholicism and perceived absolutism and William of Orange invited by Parliament to occupy the vacant throne, effectively signalled the triumph of the covenant theory of monarchy over that of divine right. The interruption in the succession which brought William and his wife Mary to the throne and the conditionality imposed on their accession broke two of the cardinal principles of divine right theory. The Glorious Revolution, as it came to be known, replaced the iconography and mystery of Stuart sacred kingship with a monarchy more prosaic, popular and Protestant. Significantly, William of Orange had little time for the ritual of touching for the king's evil, telling one sufferer who approached him for a cure, 'God give you better health, and more sense.'[7]

The constitutional settlement that followed the Glorious Revolution rested on a concept of limited monarchy where sovereignty lay with the Crown in Parliament. It was based on an essentially secular Whig concept of social and civil contract, as propounded in the writings of John Locke. After 1689 there were far fewer appeals by either monarchs or churchmen to Old Testament texts and the model of Israelite kingship. In Oliver O'Donovan's words, 'The ruler's primary responsibility ceased to be thought of as being to divine law, but rather to the people whose supposed act constituted him.[8] However, neither the notion of the godly prince ruling the godly commonwealth nor the close connections between Crown and Church were swept away. In two respects, indeed, they were strengthened. The link between the monarch and the established churches of England and Scotland, the former Anglican and the latter now Presbyterian (because Episcopalians in Scotland had refused to recognize William and Mary and maintained their loyalty to the exiled James as they did to his Jacobite successors), and the emphatic Protestantism of the United Kingdom monarchy were both confirmed. One of the conditions on which William had been offered the throne was that he would outlaw episcopacy in Scotland and maintain the Presbyterian government of the Church of Scotland. In England he retained the position of Supreme Governor of the established church. The coronation oath was recast so that the sovereign now promised to maintain not just the laws of God, and the true profession of the Gospel, but also 'the Protestant Reformed Religion established by law' (see page 135).

Divine Providence

If the sovereign was now seen as being accountable as much to the people through Parliament as to God, there was still a strong sense of the divine ordination of the institution of monarchy. In place of the theory of divine right to which the Stuarts had appealed, the Hanoverian dynasty was sustained by a notion of divine providence, which saw Britain as a chosen nation over whom God had placed a Protestant ruler.

Perhaps the supreme artistic representations of this idea are to be found in the ceiling and wall murals in the Royal Naval Hospital in Greenwich painted between 1707 and 1725. The ceiling of the main hall depicts the triumph of peace and liberty over the forces of tyranny. William and Mary sit enthroned in heaven surrounded by the cardinal virtues with William being handed an olive branch by Peace, surrounded by her doves and lambs, while himself presenting the red cap of liberty to the kneeling figure of Europe. On the west wall under the Latin inscription '*Iam Nova Progenes Coelo*' (And Now for a New Race from Heaven) Britain's first Hanoverian monarch, George I, is shown surrounded by his Protestant heirs with the dome of St Paul's Cathedral behind him and Providence descending from heaven to put the sceptre of sovereignty into his hands. A similar message is conveyed in the opening line of the patriotic song, 'Rule, Britannia', written around 1740, which speaks of Britain arising 'at heaven's command'.

National Anthem

Ironically, The British national anthem, which stands as one of the most abiding monuments to the whole project of Protestant monarchy, may well have had Jacobite and Catholic origins. 'God save great James our king' was sung by Stuart loyalists on the eve of William of Orange's invasion. At what stage this Stuart anthem was appropriated for the Hanoverians is not clear but it was undoubtedly the threat of the Jacobite rebellion in 1745 that brought it into the public domain. 'God Save great George our King' received its first known public performance at the

Theatre Royal, Drury Lane, on 28 September 1745 following the manager's announcement that he was raising a troop of soldiers to fight for the king with his actors as its nucleus. 'God save the king' seems first to have been sung in churches during George III's bouts of illness when verses were added praying for the king's deliverance and thanking God for his recovery. The first coronation to include the national anthem was that of George IV in 1821 and by Victoria's reign it had become the invariable accompaniment to public appearances by the sovereign.

The national anthem was a peculiarly British invention, rapidly copied by other countries, twenty of which at one time or another adopted or adapted its tune for their own national songs. What distinguished the British version was the fact it was so clearly addressed to God rather than to the fatherland, the flag or some other symbol and that it focused very directly on the person of the sovereign rather than on the nation or people. While it clearly called on the Almighty to bless and protect the monarch, however, there was no hint of divine right theory.

Protestant virtues

The late eighteenth century saw the monarchy's continuing appeal resting not on notions of divine right or sacred kingship but rather on respect and affection for those who occupied the throne and for their exercise of what might be thought of as characteristic Protestant virtues. The reign of George III was pivotal in this respect, inspiring a new popular reverence for monarchy based on the king's earnestness, conscientious exercise of his duties and absolute propriety. To some these might seem dull if worthy characteristics but for the many influenced by the Evangelical Revival which had brought a new mood of seriousness across the country, there was something both reassuring and even endearing about the fact that the monarch prayed regularly, was loyal to his wife, and behaved in a sober and solid way. George III and Queen Charlotte established a paradigm of happy and fruitful royal marriage which was to help maintain public respect and affection for the British monarchy after it ceased to have any major political role or influence.

They also pioneered another important role of the modern British monarchy in their patronage and direct support of voluntary, philanthropic and charitable endeavours. Frank Prochaska traces the origins of what he calls Britain's 'welfare monarchy' to their activities and notes that they both distributed proportionately more of their own wealth to charitable purposes than any other British sovereign.[32] They especially favoured the Christian-inspired charitable societies established in the wake of the Evangelical Revival to promote missionary endeavour, education, poor relief, moral reform and the abolition of slavery. In their turn, leading figures in the revival like Hannah More extolled the Crown as the focus of national morality and also commended its Christ-like assumption of sacrificial dedication and service:

> *A Crown! What is it?*
> *It is to bear the miseries of a people!*
> *To hear their murmurs, feel their discontents,*
> *And sink beneath a load of splendid care!* [9]

As well as associating the Crown with domestic virtue and propriety, George III consciously promoted its more splendid and majestic elements. He rebuilt Buckingham Palace as a spectacular royal residence and centre for court ceremonial in London and went on frequent royal visits around the country, displaying the public face of monarchy to the people in a way that has been followed by all subsequent sovereigns. Several of his public appearances involved religious ceremonies and church services, as when he led the nation in thanking God for the victorious outcome of the Napoleonic wars. This, too, established an important precedent in linking the crown in public perception with church attendance and significant sacred occasions.

Victoria

Those same royal values which George III exemplified – respectability, philanthropy, religious commitment, private morality and public duty – characterized the life and reign of his grand-daughter, Queen Victoria. Her own deep faith was a powerful spur in the way she conceived her role as a Christian monarch. When her ministers submitted a royal proclamation to the people of India in 1859 she was appalled to find that it made no mention of God or the Christian religion and took up her pen to add at the beginning of the document the phrase 'Firmly relying on the truth of Christianity, and acknowledging with gratitude the solace of religion' and, at the end, 'May the God of all power grant to us, and those in authority under us, strength to carry out these, our wishes, for the good of our people.' [10]

Although her own natural shyness and reserve and her low churchmanship inclined her to eschew large and showy religious observances, there was one area in which Victoria did echo the appeal of earlier monarchs to the traditions of sacred kingship, its Old Testament origins and its visualization and representation in concrete form. She commemorated the deaths of those closest to her with elaborate monuments filled with morally uplifting and improving images. Perhaps the most striking of these eloquent sermons in stone is the chapel at Windsor which she fitted out as a memorial to Albert after his death in 1861. The Albert Chapel stands as a magnificent testament to the ideal of Christian monarchy. There are striking murals of Moses blessing the Israelites and Solomon receiving the gifts of the kings of the earth. A bas-relief depicts the wisdom of Solomon and the theme of sacrifice is underlined by panels showing the betrayal, arrest and crucifixion of Christ, the bound figure of Isaac and the symbol of the pelican. The Prince Consort's cenotaph is surrounded by statues of the principal saints of the British Isles together with the Virgin Mary and St Michael the Archangel. The immense mausoleum which Victoria ordered to be built at Frogmore to house Albert's remains further emphasized the sanctity of monarchy and proclaimed the Queen's sure and certain Christian faith, not least through the text which she chose to have inscribed above the entrance doors: 'Farewell, best beloved, here at last I shall rest with thee, with thee in Christ I shall rise'.

The level of grief and the certainty of meeting again in heaven which characterised Victoria's mourning for Albert hugely influenced her subjects' attitudes to death and the afterlife. She created a new role for the monarch as chief mourner for the nation. In this and in other ways she epitomized the central argument of Walter Bagehot's classic work,

The English Constitution, published almost halfway through her reign in 1867, that, lacking political power, modern monarchy would survive and indeed thrive by appealing to the heart rather than the head. 'So long as the human heart is strong and the human reason weak,' Bagehot wrote, 'Royalty will be strong because it appeals to diffused feeling, and Republics weak because they appeal to the understanding.'[11] He commended the situation prevailing in his own time whereby the Crown had come to be regarded as 'the head of both our society and morality':

> The virtues of Queen Victoria and the virtues of George III have sunk deep into the popular heart. We have come to believe that it is natural to have a virtuous sovereign, and that the domestic virtues are as likely to be found on thrones as they are eminent when there. [12]

Bagehot's perceptive observations on the value and purpose of modern monarchy were studied by both George V and George VI. 'Commonly hidden like a mystery, and sometimes paraded like a pageant', he wrote, it 'consecrates our whole state'. The key was to preserve the balance between maintaining the mystery and parading the pageantry, something that was achieved in the late Victorian and Edwardian period by increasingly public and splendid ceremonial. David Cannadine has pointed to the decisive change that took place in the image of the British monarchy in the period between the late 1870s and 1914.[13] Its ritual and ceremonial aspects, which had hitherto been largely low-key, private, often ineptly organised and of little popular appeal became splendid, public and popular.

Victoria's longevity encouraged the Church of England to organise large-scale services to celebrate her golden and diamond jubilees and bask in her reflected glory. For the service in 1887 to mark the fiftieth anniversary of her accession, Westminster Abbey was transformed by the rebuilding of the organ, the remodelling of the choir stalls and the introduction of electric lighting. The officiating clergy were dressed for the first time in copes and coloured stoles, hailed by a journalist present as 'a novel and picturesque innovation'. Church and Crown were indissolubly linked and jointly promoted. Edward Benson, the Archbishop of Canterbury took the cheering crowds who greeted the Queen as she drove through the East End of London as an indicator that both institutions were loved and valued by the English people. 'They are not a church-going race', he noted in his diary, 'but there is a solemn quiet sense of religion for all that in their sayings and doings.' [14]

The Windsors

The pattern of Christian monarchy established by Victoria and predicated on the values of duty, discretion and dignity held throughout the twentieth century and is still largely normative today. As practised by the Windsors, it has had four main prongs: civic duty expressed principally through philanthropic and charitable activity; spiritual leadership demonstrated through attendance at religious services and public exhortation; the development of ceremonial and ritual to emphasize the splendid and mystical aspects of monarchy; and personal example through private lives lived according to high moral principles and family values, although this last aspect has not always been maintained.

The Edwardian era, traditionally associated with the full flowering of British imperialism, saw a conscious revival of the chivalric aspects of medieval Christian kingship. The investiture of the future Edward VIII as Prince of Wales in Carnarfon Castle in 1911, a wholly novel event packed with medieval language and symbolism, was infused with Christian references. The 17-year-old prince ended his speech saying (in Welsh) 'Without God, without anything; God is enough'. Imperialism encouraged reverential feelings towards the monarchy, as exemplified in the 1911 Indian Durbar where George V appeared to a quarter of a million of his Indian subjects as 'a semi-divine figure' clad in purple robes and wearing a crown valued at £60,000. It also inspired a revival of the medieval system of knightly honours and orders of chivalry centred on and deriving from the person of the monarch. The Order of the British Empire was instituted in 1917 to embrace the 99 per cent of the population who did not qualify for the medieval orders of the Garter, Thistle and Bath, and to honour especially those involved in philanthropic work, literature, science and art. Modelled on the old chivalric orders, it had an explicitly Christian focus, expressed in its motto 'For God and the Empire' and the fact that it had both a prelate, the Bishop of London, and a chapel (eventually) in the crypt of St Paul's Cathedral.

The close association of the Crown with the values of heroic sacrifice and knightly virtue was confirmed in the First World War and perhaps supremely expressed in the funeral of the unknown warrior in Westminster Abbey in 1920 when King George V walked behind the coffin on which a wreath bore a card written in his own hand (see page 215). In the words of Piers Brendon and Phillip Whitehead, 'The funeral was a consecration of chivalry whose apotheosis was the Crown'. The inscription on the tomb concluded, 'They buried him among the kings because he had done good towards God and towards his house.' [15]

The years following the First World War saw a significant shift in the arrangements made for royal weddings and funerals. Hitherto largely private affairs, taking place in one of the royal chapels, they became big state occasions focused on a church service in Westminster Abbey or St Paul's Cathedral. Edward VII was the first monarch to lie in state after his death in 1910. The wedding of Princess Mary and Viscount Lascelles in 1922 took place not in the privacy of the chapel at St James's Palace or Windsor but in Westminster Abbey with a procession through the streets of London beforehand. The following year the Duke of York became the first royal prince to be married in the Abbey for five hundred years. Since then, virtually all royal weddings have taken place in one of the two major Anglican churches in London with spectacular processions through the capital, their national profile and reach enhanced by radio and television coverage.

Westminster Abbey and St Paul's Cathedral have also been the venues for other highly visible services where monarchs have given thanks for particular anniversaries or led the nation in acts of thanksgiving or remembrance. George V was an enthusiastic and active participant in the service at St Paul's which marked the high point of his silver jubilee celebrations in 1935. In an address relayed through loudspeakers to the cheering multitude outside, the Archbishop of Canterbury declared that the national spirit of unity had found its centre in the throne and that the king was 'the Father of his People'. The king and queen appeared on the balcony of Buckingham Palace every night for a week to acknowledge the raptuorous applause of the crowds below and drove through the East End and docklands of London. The spiritual dimension of the jubilee celebrations was commented on by several of those who took part. After attending a reception for Dominion Prime Ministers, the Labour politician Ramsay Macdonald noted 'We all went away feeling that we had taken part in something very much like a Holy Communion.' [16]

There have been wobbles of course, like the Abdication of 1936, but they did not do lasting damage. George VI restored decency, dignity, self-discipline and conscientiousness to the Crown, not least through exercising his own deep Christian faith. *The Times* leader on the morning of his coronation noted that successful kingship relies 'not upon intellectual brilliance or superlative talent of any kind, but upon the moral qualities of steadiness, staying-power and self-sacrifice'.[17] It was on similar foundations that Elizabeth II based her reign, exemplifying the qualities of wisdom, faithfulness and unstinting and devoted public service. On a number of occasions she emphasized the importance of spiritual values in an increasingly secular society. It was at her insistence that the fiftieth anniversary of her accession to the throne in 2002 should be marked primarily by church services and seen as an occasion for religious observance as well as partying. Her diamond and platinum jubilees were celebrated by exuberant multi-faith and multi-cultural carnival processions and pop concerts but both had Christian services of thanksgiving at their centre.

The increasing focus on the personalities and morals of individual monarchs and of the wider royal family, which has resulted from the change of direction initiated by George III and Victoria and been exacerbated by the relentless prying and prurience of the media, carries a high risk. It threatens to turn the royals into celebrities and also means that those who fail to live up to high standards of behaviour debase the standing of the institution. Yet Bagehot was right in saying that monarchy's appeal is to the heart rather than the head and that it connects with the emotions rather than with reason. This is pre-eminently true of its sacred aspects and has perhaps nowhere been more evident than in the aftermath of royal deaths. In his book, *Great Deaths*, John Wolffe points to the spontaneous gathering of crowds in public places that followed the deaths of Princess Charlotte in 1817 and Prince Albert in 1861 and notes more generally that throughout the nineteenth and twentieth centuries royal deaths 'drew people to church in unusually high numbers and also stirred prolific religious and quasi-religious discourse'.[18] This was also true following the sudden death of Diana, Princess of Wales, in 1997 and, as discussed in the introduction to this book, Elizabeth II's death in 2022 similarly unleashed a latent religiosity in the British people. In both cases, there was something positively medieval in the shrines that were created and the public displays of grief, testaments to the continuing spiritual appeal and sacred character of monarchy.

PART 3
The Coronation

It is the coronation more than any other event that underlines the sacred nature of the United Kingdom monarchy. Packed with religious symbolism and imagery, it exudes mystery and magic, binds together church and state through the person of the monarch and clearly proclaims the derivation of all power and authority from God and the Christian basis on which government is exercised, justice administered and the state defended. At their coronations kings and queens are not simply crowned and enthroned but consecrated, set apart and anointed, dedicated to God and invested with sacerdotal garb and symbolic regalia. Here, if anywhere, we find the divinity which hedges the throne.

The United Kingdom is the only country which still marks the accession of a new monarch with a coronation. Of the other European monarchies, Belgium, Luxembourg and the Netherlands have never held coronations, Spain discontinued them in 1492 (they were not revived when the monarchy was restored there in 1975), Denmark in 1849 and Sweden in 1873. Norway abolished coronations in 1908 although since then its monarchs have undergone a ceremony of consecration or blessing in Nidaros Cathedral, Trondheim, with the royal regalia present in the church but not used in the ceremony.

Coronations are religious services rather than constitutional ceremonies. The next three chapters explore their origins and historical development, key elements and symbolism, and the way they have been interpreted by both religious and secular commentators.

Chapter 6

THE ORIGINS AND HISTORICAL DEVELOPMENT OF THE CORONATION

The coronation service has been subtly adapted over the centuries but has essentially retained the same basic format for over a thousand years. The crowning and enthronement of the monarch is just one of several distinct elements in the service. Others include recognition by the assembled congregation representing the people of their new sovereign, administration of oaths, anointing with holy oil, investiture with the royal regalia and celebration of Holy Communion. All these elements are present in the earliest surviving order for the coronation of an English monarch, prepared by St Dunstan as Archbishop of Canterbury in 973, and were almost certainly found in earlier coronations.

The Old Testament influence

The inauguration ceremonies for the kings of Israel as described in the Old Testament have provided the model and template for all Christian coronations in Britain. The most solemn moment in the coronation service, the anointing of the new monarch with holy oil, is directly derived from the anointing of Solomon and accompanied by the singing of verses from 1 Kings 1: 'Zadok the priest and Nathan the prophet anointed Solomon king; and all the people rejoiced and said: God save the king, Long live the king, May the king live for ever. Amen. Hallelujah.' Since 1727 these words have been sung to G. F. Handel's thrilling setting written for the coronation of George II. Coronation sermons have frequently contained references to Solomon, and also to David and Josiah. The one preached at Charles II's Scottish coronation at Scone in 1651 also mentioned Saul, Joash, Ahaziah, Asa, Hezekiah and even the wicked queen Athaliah to whom Charles's mother was compared.

The strong Old Testament influence is also evident in the centrality of the covenant theme in British coronations. Through the solemn oaths sworn near the beginning of the service and the act of homage towards the end, God, monarch and people are bound together in a three-way covenant. Not surprisingly, the psalms have long played a prominent part in coronation services. Settings by Handel of the opening verses of Psalm 21, 'The king shall rejoice', and verses from Psalm 89, 'Let thy hand be strengthened' were sung as the opening and closing anthems at the coronations of George II and George III. Elizabeth II's coronation began with the opening verses of Psalm 122, 'I was glad when they said unto me, we will go to the house of the Lord', set to the majestic tune written by Hubert Parry for the coronation of Edward VII in 1902.

The development of coronation services based on the Old Testament model played a key role in the transition from primal sacred kingship to Christian monarchy. Crownings and enthronements were a central feature of pre-Christian kingship and they often involved rituals indicating the divinity of the new monarch. With the coming of Christianity, kings were no longer seen as gods. Through being anointed at their coronations, however, they were set apart and given quasi-priestly status. Much reference was made to Melchizedek as the model priest-king in early Christian coronation orders and as late as 1308 he was explicitly cited as the model for the king of England. The priestly, and even episcopal, attributes of the monarch remained a significant theme in the coronation service but the emphasis shifted from the Melchizedekian model of the priest king to the notion of the monarch as one who rules by the grace and through the authority of God.

While preserving the concept of popular choice, symbolised by the act of recognition at the beginning of the service, the Christian coronation emphasized the monarch's crowning by God rather than by people. As such it easily accommodated and, indeed, facilitated the transition from popular election to hereditary succession which occurred in both Celtic and Anglo-Saxon monarchy. In Christian coronations, the focus was not on choosing a king, or even crowning and enthroning him, but rather on invoking the divine blessing, setting him apart and reminding him of the derivation of his power from God and his responsibility to rule wisely, justly and mercifully. Christian consecration took over from constitutional investiture as the main function of the coronation ceremony which came to be seen as a religious service for which the monarch prepared with spiritual reflection and prayer and which usually took place in the context of a celebration of Holy Communion. Orders of services which have survived from the archives of Egbert, during whose time as Archbishop of York from 734 to 766 four kings acceded to the Northumbrian throne, include what is described as 'Mass for Kings on the day of their Benediction'.

Earliest accounts of the blessing and ordination of kings

Before full-scale coronations came to be introduced into the British Isles in the tenth century, there were Christian inauguration ceremonies variously described as benedictions, ordinations or consecrations. It is not clear when the first such ceremony took place. Gildas, a Welsh monk writing in the sixth century, speaks about the unction or anointing of British kings ruling after the withdrawal of the Romans. Adomnán tells of Columba being three times visited by an angel commanding him to ordain Aedán to the kingship of Dál Riata according to the rubrics laid down in a glass book. If he is to be believed, the ordination which Columba duly performed on Iona in 574, by laying his hand on Aedán's head and blessing him, is the first clearly recorded Christian inauguration ceremony for a monarch not just in the British Isles but anywhere in Europe. A purple passage in *The Times'* special supplement on the 1937 coronation noted that 'our first remote glimpse of the consecration of a king on British soil is by a ray of dim religious light falling upon the sacred isle of Iona'. A monograph by Michael Enright casts doubt on the historicity of Adomnán's account, written a hundred years after the events it describes, and suggests that he invented the story of Aedán's ordination by Columba in order to bolster the concept of Christian kingship in general and more specifically to support the claim of the abbots of Iona in his own time to consecrate the kings of Dál Riata.[1]

Even if this is the case, by the late-seventh century abbots of Iona do seem to have been consecrating the kings of Dál Riata, using Columba's supposed ordination of Aedán as a precedent. The ceremony almost took place on the summit of the rocky crag of Dunadd in mid-Argyll, the site of pre-Christian inauguration rites, where the king placed his foot in a specially carved indentation in the rock to signal his marriage to the land and the continuity of his succession. It blended Christian and pre-Christian elements, with a priest presiding but the king still placing his foot in the rock-cut footprint. Similar outdoor inauguration and coronation ceremonies for monarchs across the British Isles remained common until the Norman Conquest. Kings continued to be crowned sitting on stones, chosen for their symbolic strength and stability. The coronation stone at Kingston upon Thames was used for the crowning of Christian Anglo-Saxon kings, as it had been for their pagan predecessors, kings of Munster were crowned on the rock of Cashel, and the stone of Scone was almost certainly used for all Scottish coronations from that of Kenneth MacAlpin in the mid-ninth century until its removal to England by Edward I in 1296.

Anointing

While the earliest Christian ceremonies for blessing and consecrating new monarchs do not appear to have involved anointing with holy oil, this came to be a key element, following the precedent of the anointing of Israelite kings and symbolizing the descent of the Holy Spirit . The first Christian king in Europe to have been anointed may have been Wamba of Spain in 672. Historians are generally agreed that full-scale Christian inauguration rites for monarchs involving ecclesiastical blessing and anointing in the context of a proper liturgical service were probably developed in the eighth century by the Merovingians, drawing on earlier Byzantine practices in the Eastern Roman Empire. Some maintain that the first well-attested anointing of a European monarch did not take place until 751 when the Frankish king Pippin, having been elected king of the Franks by an assembly of nobles, was anointed in a ceremony in Soissons which may well have been influenced by Adomnán's account of Columba's ordination of Aedán. He received a second anointing from Pope Stephen II in a lavish ceremony at the Basilica of St Denis in Paris three years later. The first documented royal anointing in England is that of Ecgfith, the son of Offa, who was anointed king of Mercia by visiting papal legates in 787. The practice of anointing kings was largely confined to England, Ireland, France and Sicily. It does not seem to have been taken up in Scotland until 1331 when David II was crowned and anointed, apparently in response to a request from Robert the Bruce and according to the terms of a Bull from Pope John XXI.

Crowning

While pre-Christian practices of enthronement and investiture with weapons and regalia were incorporated into the new Christian services of monarchical inauguration, other new elements distinguished them from what had gone before. Anointing was the most significant with its sacerdotal connotations but another important symbolic step in the Christianising of royal inauguration rituals was the replacement of the traditional warrior's helmet by a *corona* or crown. From the time of the Roman Emperor Constantine in the early fourth century, the soldier's torque, similar to those worn round the neck, was replaced by a crown or diadem for imperial coronations. Murals and mosaics depict emperors being crowned by a heavenly hand, perhaps echoing depictions in early Christian art of martyrs being crowned from heaven. The crown preserved the association with sacrifice found in the shamanistic torque, introduced Christian notions of martyrdom and drew on imagery found in both the Old and New Testaments. Some scholars suggest that it derives from the rays of glory which played around the head of Moses on his descent from Mount Sinai. The action of Pope Leo III in placing a crown of the head of the Holy Roman Emperor Charlemagne on 25 December 800 clearly signalled the church's takeover of the imperial inauguration process.

There is some doubt as to when the first crowning of an English king took place but it was probably either of Alfred's son, Edward the Elder, in 901 or of Athelstan in 925, both ceremonies taking place at Kingston upon Thames.

The earliest surviving coronation orders

The first English coronation of which both a clear record and a full order survive was that of Edgar in Bath Abbey in 973, fourteen years after his accession to the throne. The long delay may be explained by the desire of the church to wait until he was thirty-one, the age at which priesting took place. His coronation, which was held on Whit Sunday, the traditional day for ordinations to the priesthood, laid considerable emphasis on the theme of consecration and the sacerdotal aspects of kingship. Bedecked with the roses of martyrdom and the lilies of chastity and clad in priestly robes, he was anointed and crowned by Dunstan, Archbishop of Canterbury, entrusted with the protection and supervision of the church and graced with the titles *rex dei gratia* and *vicarus dei*. His wife, Aelfthryth, was anointed and crowned as queen at the same ceremony. This practice, of a double crowning and anointing, was followed in the coronations of all subsequent married kings and queens.

The order drawn up by Dunstan, which seems to have borrowed from Carolingian and Frankish rites as well as indigenous Celtic and Anglo-Saxon practices, contained many of the key elements found in all subsequent English coronations. Edgar was led by hand into Bath Abbey by two bishops and prostrated himself in front of the altar while the Archbishop intoned the *Te Deum*. The three oaths which he was required to swear were similar to those administered by Archbishop Egbert of York more than two hundred years earlier, when the king swore that 'the Church of God and all Christian people keep true peace at every time', that 'he forbids all robberies and all iniquities unto all degrees' and that 'he commands righteousness and mercy in all judgments'. Dunstan's *Ordo* also included anointing with a mixture of oil and balsam poured from an animal's horn while the anthem 'Zadok the Priest and Nathan the Prophet' was sung, enthronement, crowning and investiture of the monarch with a ring, sword, sceptre and staff or *baculus*. The queen was similarly anointed and crowned and Mass was celebrated. At the close of the service all those present hailed the king with the words, *'Vivat rex'*, and the nobles bound themselves to their new ruler by a kiss. Dunstan's *Ordo* clearly established clerical control over royal inauguration rites in England, and specifically the key role of the Archbishop of Canterbury in presiding over the ceremony.

A full record also survives of a second coronation over which Dunstan presided, that of Ethelred II, known as Ethelred the Unready, at Kingston upon Thames in 979. At his baptism, which had also been at the hands of Dunstan, the infant Ethelred had caused some consternation by urinating into the font but there were no such mishaps at his coronation service which was similar to Edgar's and full of Old Testament references. The opening prayer of consecration, at which the crown was held over the king's head, invoked the coronation of David and asked that Ethelred might have 'the faithfulness of Abraham, the meekness of Moses, the courage of Joshua, the humility of David and the wisdom of Solomon.' The prayer of anointing began, 'O Christ, anoint this king with the power with which thou hast anointed priests, kings, prophets and martyrs.'[2] In his sermon Dunstan preached on the duties of a consecrated king, describing him as the shepherd over his people and reminding him that while ruling justly would earn him 'worship in this world' as well as God's mercy, any departure from his duties would lead to punishment at Doomsday.

The move to Westminster Abbey

Harold Godwinson, also called Harold II, the last Anglo-Saxon English king, who came to the throne in January 1066, was almost certainly the first English monarch to be crowned in Westminster Abbey, which had been built by his predecessor Edward the Confessor. Following his defeat in the Battle of Hastings, he was succeeded nine months later by William the Conqueror who was also crowned there and it has remained the venue for the coronation of subsequent English and United Kingdom monarchs.

The Norman Conquest brought a more settled succession with the hereditary principle replacing election and choice by nobles. This confirmed the function of the coronation as a religious service in which a monarch whose accession was already secure was consecrated and given divine blessing. Orders used for the coronation of Norman kings broadly followed Dunstan's Anglo-Saxon *Ordo*. William I was crowned by Aldred, Archbishop of York, but after some wrangling in the twelfth century the principle was established that only the Archbishop of Canterbury was entitled to crown the king and queen. The sacred significance of coronations was underlined by the fact that several were held on major Christian feast days following the precedent of Edgar's on Whit Sunday. Edward the Confessor's was on Easter Sunday, William I's on Christmas Day and King John's on Ascension Day.

Medieval coronations

Medieval coronations emphasised the priestly nature of kingship, as described in an anonymous tract written at the time of Henry II's coronation in 1154:

Kings are consecrated in God's church before the sacred altar and are anointed with holy oil and sacred benediction to exercise ruling power over Christians.... Wherefore he is not called a layman, since he is anointed of the Lord and through grace he is God. He is the supreme ruler, the chief shepherd, master, defender and instructor of the Holy Church, the chief and supreme prelate.[3]

Henry IV was described at his coronation as being 'apparelled like a prelate of the church' and Henry VI as 'arrayed like as a bishop should say mass with a dalmatic and a stole about his neck'.[4]

A beautifully illuminated service book, the *Liber Regalis*, drawn up for the coronation of Richard II in 1377 and preserved in the library of Westminster Abbey, came to supplant Dunstan's *Ordo*, which it followed closely in most respects, and has been used as the basis for all subsequent coronations with only relatively minor modifications being made. Most of the alterations that have been made are in respect of the oaths which were based on those taken by Edward I in 1308. As prescribed in the *Liber Regalis*, and translated into modern English, the oaths bound the monarch to 'grant and preserve the laws and customs granted by ancient, just and God-fearing kings to the people of England', to 'preserve intact the peace of the Church of God for the clergy and people', to 'ensure in all judgements equal and true justice and discretion in mercy and truth' and to 'grant that just laws and customs which the people shall have chosen are to be observed'.

With ever more elaborate staging being erected in the Abbey crossing, late medieval coronations achieved a level of spectacle and theatricality which is well conveyed by the art historian Roy Strong:

> The monarch arrived, ascended to the pulpitum in his robes of state and sat on high in the literal sense, for the stage or scaffold was at least thirteen feet high. He then descended down the other side to the sacrarium next to the altar, was partially stripped and then, hidden from the gaze of the onlookers by a pall, anointed. After this he was vested in robes which were virtually all ancient holy relics, seated in the coronation chair (first certainly used in 1399) and crowned. He then 'ascended' in full magnificence, like a glittering icon, and was led up the great flight of steps to be enthroned on a chair which was up a further flight. The effect of his epiphany on those groundlings in the transepts seeing this figure from afar almost floating 25 feet above them must have been electrifying.[5]

Tudor and Stuart coronations

Following the Reformation there was a switch of emphasis from the priestly to kingly aspects of monarchy, in technical terms from *sacerdotium* to *regnum*, although vestments associated with priests and bishops continued to be worn by monarchs at their coronations. Anointing remained the central and most scared element in the service although there were slight changes to how it was administered. The *Liber Regalis* had laid down that there should be two *ampullae*, as the anointing vessels are known, one containing pure oil and the other a holy chrism made of olive oil and balm. Tudor monarchs received

a double anointing but since Stuart times a mixture
of oil and balm in a single *ampulla* has been used.
Early English coronation orders seem simply to
have provided for the monarch to be anointed on
the crown of the head, but later a fivefold anointing
ritual was used, involving the hands, breast, shoulder,
elbows and head. The boy king Edward VI was laid
on the altar so that Archbishop Cranmer could
anoint his back. From 1685 anointing has been
reduced to the hands, breast and crown of the head,
although at Queen Victoria's coronation anointing
on the breast was omitted 'from motives of delicacy'.
Later Plantagenet and Tudor monarchs knelt to be
anointed but since the coronation of Charles I it has
been customary for the sovereign to remain seated.

Most of the Stuart monarchs had a double
coronation, with three being crowned separately in
Scotland and England. James Charles, the only son of
Mary Queen of Scots, and the first British sovereign
to bear more than one Christian name, was crowne d
James VI of Scotland at Stirling in 1590, and James I of
England in London in 1603. Charles I was crowned at
Westminster Abbey in 1626, and at Holyrood Abbey,
Edinburgh, in 1633 in the only Scottish coronation
to have used the rites of the Church of England. The
order was reversed in the case of Charles II, who
was crowned at Scone Abbey on New Year's Day
1651 in a Presbyterian service where there was no
anointing and at Westminster Abbey on St George's
Day 1661 (all English Stuart coronations took place
on this day). James II also had two coronations,
being crowned and anointed in a private Roman
Catholic service in his chapel at Whitehall the
day before his coronation at Westminster Abbey at
which the celebration of communion was omitted.

All subsequent British sovereigns have had a single coronation in Westminster Abbey in the context of a service of Holy Communion according to the rites of the Church of England.

Doubtless partly inspired by the doctrine of the Divine Right of Kings, Stuart coronations were particularly splendid and perhaps came close to committing the besetting British sin of monarcholatry and turning earthly sovereigns into gods. Charles II was advised by one of his courtiers on the eve of his London coronation to 'show yourself glorious to your people, like a God' and compared in one of the many adulatory poems penned for the occasion to Jove amidst the gods, Saul crowned, the sun on Easter Sunday, Apollo the great 'Lord of Light', Christ as king, priest and prophet, and St Paul finishing the race and gaining his crown.[6]

Coronations since 1689

Apart from changes in the wording of the coronation oaths, there have been relatively few changes to the substance or ordering of coronations over the last 300 or more years. The Old Testament accounts of the anointing of Israelite kings and the rubrics of Dunstan's *Ordo* and the *Liber Regalis* have remained the templates and there has been little change in the liturgical language, the pomp or the pageantry with most of the innovations coming in the form of specially composed music. George II's coronation in 1727 featured four anthems specially composed by Handel, including 'Zadok the Priest'. It was also notable for the fact that the Queen's dress was so encrusted with jewels that a pulley had to be set up to lift her skirt when she knelt. The presentation of the Bible to the new monarch by the Archbishop of Canterbury was introduced into the coronation service in 1689. At Queen Elizabeth II's coronation in 1953 the presentation was made by the Moderator of the General Assembly of the Church of Scotland, the only non-Anglican cleric so far to have taken part in a post-Reformation coronation service. Clement Davies, leader of the Liberal Party, suggested that the leader of the Free Church Federal Council should have a role in Elizabeth's coronation but this was vetoed by Geoffrey Fisher, the Archbishop of Canterbury.

Misdemeanours, muddles and mishaps

Not all monarchs have taken their coronations as seriously as they should. Dunstan, then abbot of Glastonbury, was appalled by the behaviour of King Eadwig immediately after his crowning and anointing at Kingston upon Thames in 955. He noted that 'the lustful man suddenly jumped up and left the happy banquet and the fitting company of his nobles for the caresses of loose women'. Dunstan and another cleric were sent to drag the king back to the ceremony. When they entered his apartments, they found the royal crown carelessly thrown down on the floor and the king wallowing between two ladies 'in evil fashion, as if in a vile sty'. He was reluctant to leave but Dunstan 'after first rebuking the folly of the women, drew him by the hand from his licentious reclining by the women, replaced the crown, and brought him with him to the royal assembly, though dragged from the women by force'.[7] King John apparently laughed throughout his coronation and refused to take communion. Richard II fell asleep halfway through the ceremony, although as he was only ten years old his exhaustion is understandable. George IV nodded and winked to his mistress, Lady Conyngham, throughout his coronation and Edward VII installed his lady friends, including Alice Keppel, Jennie Churchill and Sarah Bernhardt, in a gallery which was dubbed the 'King's loose box'.

Several coronations have been marred by disasters and mishaps which were not the fault of the monarch. During the crowning of William I the Norman cavalry outside Westminster Abbey mistook the shout of acclamation inside for a riot and proceeded to massacre a group of Saxons who had the misfortune to be in the vicinity. The oil used to anoint Elizabeth I was rancid and had a foul smell, and during James II's coronation the royal standard flying over the Tower of London tore in two and the crown would not stay firmly on the king's head. George III's coronation was a raucous and chaotic affair which lasted five hours. Copious refreshments were provided and several of those present chose to eat their lunch noisily during the anointing. Chairs for the king and queen and a canopy to cover them during the anointing failed to be provided, and the Lord Mayor had to provide his own sword as a last minute substitute for the Sword of State which the Earl Marshal had forgotten to bring. When the king was about to receive communion he asked the Archbishop of Canterbury if he should remove his crown. The Archbishop consulted with the Dean and said that they could not recall any precedent as previous monarchs had always taken communion wearing their crowns. 'Then there ought to be' George III said, removing his crown. He urged the Queen to do the same but her crown was pinned on to her hair. Subsequent monarchs have followed his example during the communion part of the coronation service.

George IV's estranged wife, Caroline, was barred from entering Westminster Abbey when she turned up for her husband's coronation in 1821. Victoria's coronation was a muddled affair in which the officiating clergy demonstrated particular ineptness. The Archbishop of Canterbury made a mess of delivering the orb to the Queen and shoved the ring on to the wrong finger, causing considerable delay and much pain. When the Queen withdrew to St Edward's Chapel after the anthem she was upset to find the altar covered with sandwiches and bottles of wine. George VI also suffered from episcopal incompetence and clumsiness at his coronation in 1937. Neither of the bishops holding the form of service for him to follow could find the right page for the coronation oaths, so the Archbishop held up his copy but covered the words of the oath with his thumb.

> The supreme moment came when the Archbishop placed St Edward's crown on my head. I had taken every precaution as I thought to see that the crown was put on the right way round, but the Dean and the Archbishop had been juggling with it so much, that I never did know whether it was right or wrong ... As I turned after leaving the Coronation Chair I was brought up all standing, owing to one of the Bishops treading on my robe. I had to tell him to get off it pretty sharply as I nearly fell down.[8]

For the most part, however, British coronations have been dignified and solemn as well as splendid and spectacular. Monarchs have prepared for them with serious reflection and prayer and seen themselves as being ordained in a priestly sense, as George VI did when he said in his coronation broadcast that he had dedicated himself to 'the Ministry of Kingship'. Those who have taken part in and watched them have seen coronations as significant and moving occasions which have enhanced both the sacred significance of the monarchy and the religious life of the nation.

Chapter 7

THE ELEMENTS AND 'PROPS' IN THE CORONATION SERVICE

Buckingham Palace's announcement of the date of King Charles III's coronation stated that 'it will reflect the monarch's role today and look towards the future, while being rooted in longstanding traditions and pageantry.' I am writing this before the occasion but it seems likely that many of the elements found in previous coronations will be there in the ceremony in Westminster Abbey on 6 May 2023, albeit in a slimmed down form. There is a general expectation that it will be a shorter and smaller affair than the coronation of Elizabeth II which lasted three hours with a congregation of over 8,200. This chapter describes the traditional structure of the coronation service and the 'props' used in it, which include a special chair, a stone, four changes of costume and the royal regalia. It is based on what happened at the last coronation on 2 June 1953 so cannot be taken as an exact guide to what will happen at the next one.

The 'theatre'

Much of the coronation service takes place on a raised platform, known as 'the theatre', erected for the purpose in the crossing between the Abbey nave and the transepts. It is believed that Henry III designed this large space with coronations specifically in mind. The name of the platform points to the theatrical nature of the coronation which, like all religious services, is in a very real sense a performance in which sacred ritual and drama is enacted. Having entered the Abbey via the west door, the monarch traditionally processes to the theatre wearing a crimson robe, worn in remembrance of Christ's sacrifice, and supported on one side by the Bishop of Durham and on the other by the Bishop of Bath and Wells who have taken this role since the coronation of Richard I. The earlier practice of prostration by the monarch before the high altar has been replaced in more recent coronations by kneeling.

The recognition

The first stage of the coronation service proper, the recognition, is a survival from before the days of hereditary monarchy when part of its function was to confirm the choice of new sovereign. It traditionally takes the form of the Archbishop of Canterbury and other high officers of state formally presenting the monarch to the people, represented by those present in the Abbey, by going to each corner of the theatre and asking if they are willing to do homage and service. In the words of the order of service for the 1953 coronation, 'The people signify their willingness and joy by loud and repeated acclamations, all with one voice crying out "God save Queen Elizabeth". Then the trumpets shall sound.'[1] At this point the Bible, the paten and chalice for use in Holy Communion and the royal regalia, which have been carried in procession, are placed on the altar by the Dean of Westminster.

The coronation oaths

The three coronation oaths are next read out to the monarch while seated on a chair. The first is a solemn promise to govern the peoples of the United Kingdom of Great Britain and Northern Ireland and other direct dependencies and nations of the Commonwealth 'according to their laws and customs', the second an undertaking to 'cause law and justice, in mercy, to be executed in all your judgements' and the third a commitment to maintain 'the laws of God and the true profession of the Gospel, maintain the Protestant Reformed Religion established by law and maintain and preserve inviolably the settlement of the Church of England, and the doctrine, worship, discipline and government thereof, as by law established in England'. Having assented to the oaths, Queen Elizabeth II knelt at the altar, laying her right hand on the Holy Gospel in the Bible and saying 'The things Which I have here before promised, I will perform and keep. So help me God'.[2] She then kissed the Bible before signing the oath with the pen from a silver standish.

Presentation of the Bible

The presentation of the Bible to the new monarch was introduced for the coronation of William and Mary in 1689. It was incorporated into the investiture with the royal regalia later in the service but was moved forward to this point in the 1953 coronation when it was undertaken by the Moderator of the General Assembly of the Church of Scotland with the words: 'Here is wisdom; this is the royal law; these are the lively Oracles of God.'[3]

GOD SAVE THE KING

The Beginning of the Communion Service

The anointing, crowning and enthronement of British monarchs is traditionally performed within the context of an Anglican Communion service celebrated according to the Book of Common Prayer. In 1953 the Collect for Purity and *Kyrie Eleison* were followed by a prayer asking God to grant his servant Elizabeth 'the spirit of wisdom and government, that being devoted unto thee with her whole heart, she may so wisely govern, that in her time thy Church may be in safety, and Christian devotion may continue in peace; that so persevering in good works unto the end, she may by thy mercy come to thine everlasting kingdom'. At both the 1937 and 1953 coronations, the Epistle was 1 Peter 2:13-17 ('Submit yourselves to every ordinance of man for the Lord's sake: whether it be to the king, as supreme; or unto governors … Honour all men. Love the brotherhood. Fear God. Honour the king') and the Gospel was Matthew 22:15-22 ('Render to Caesar the things which are Caesar's and unto God the things that are God's'). These readings were followed by recitation of the Nicene Creed. Twentieth-century coronations have ditched the sermon that was preached in earlier ones at this point and moved straight into the most solemn and sacred part of the whole service, the anointing, in preparation for which the monarch takes off the crimson robe worn from the beginning of the service and, dressed in a simple linen shift symbolizing humility, first kneels again before the altar before sitting for the first time in the ceremony on the Stone of Destiny slotted into King Edward's Chair, perhaps the most important and also the most bizarre of the 'props' used in the coronation.

King Edward's Chair and the Stone of Destiny

Since 1307 every English sovereign, with the exception of Mary I and Mary II, has been anointed and crowned while seated on the oak chair dedicated to Edward the Confessor and supposedly made on the orders of Edward I to accommodate the Stone of Scone which his army had looted from Scone Abbey, near Perth, in 1296. Before its spiriting away by the 'Hammer of the Scots', as Edward was known, the stone had played a key role in the coronation of Scottish kings for at least 400 years. Despite promises that it would be returned to Scotland, it remained in London until Christmas Day 1950 when four Scottish nationalist students used a crowbar to break into Westminster Abbey. They removed the stone from the chair, only for it to crash to the floor and break in two, and loaded the pieces into a borrowed Ford Anglia. Roadblocks were erected across the Cheviot Hills, closing the Anglo-Scottish border for the first time in centuries but the thieves evaded capture by burying the stone in a wood in Kent for several weeks before later driving it back to Scotland. As they crossed the border, they pulled back the coat that covered the stone and poured some whisky on it 'signifying its return to the Celtic people'.

The stolen stone was wrapped in a saltire and left in the ruins of Arbroath Abbey where a declaration had been signed 1320 asking the Pope to recognize Scottish independence. It was returned to Westminster Abbey in 1952 and in 1996 the UK Government decreed that it should finally be returned to Scotland, with the understanding that it would be brought back to London for future coronations. Currently housed in Edinburgh Castle, it will come south for Charles III's coronation and will thereafter be on permanent display in a new museum in Perth to be opened in 2024.

This relatively insignificant piece of red sandstone, weighing about 350 lbs, cracked through the middle as a result of its abduction and decorated only by a very simple cross, carries a huge weight of religious symbolism and its legendary history illustrates well the sacred aura surrounding the British monarchy. Even Oliver Cromwell had himself installed as Lord Protector seated on the coronation throne and the stone of Scone.

Legend has it that the Stone of Scone, or Stone of Destiny as it is sometimes called, started life as the pillow on which Jacob slept when he had his dream of the ladder leading up to heaven as described in Genesis 28:12-17. The biblical story recounts that after rising early in the morning, Jacob took the stone that he had put under his head and set it up for a pillar, having poured oil on top of it. He called the place where God had delivered his promise to the descendants of Abraham Bethel. Many years later God told Jacob to return to Bethel where he renamed him Israel and said, 'a nation and a company of nations shall come from you, and kings shall spring from you' (Genesis 35.11). Again Jacob set up a pillar of stone in the place where God had spoken to him and poured oil on it. Some stories identify this with the pillar beside which Abimelech was crowned king of Israel and Josiah made his covenant with the Lord to keep his commandments and statutes.

The next chapter in the legendary history of the coronation stone provides an origin legend for the Scots and forges a link between Old Testament kingship, the pharaohs of Egypt and the kings of Ireland. There are various versions of the story. One recounts that around 580 BC, when the Babylonians under King Nebuchadnezar were invading Israel, the prophet Jeremiah and King Zedekiah's daughter, Tea, the last survivor of the Davidic line, smuggled the sacred stone out of Israel so that it would not fall into the hands of the Babylonian invaders. They went first to Egypt as guests of the Pharaoh and then via Spain to Ireland where Tea married Eochaid, king of Ireland, and took the name Scota. According to another version, the stone remained for some time in Egypt where it became the property of the country's rulers before being taken to Spain by Scota, Pharaoh's daughter, and subsequently to Ireland by one of her descendants, Simon Brek. This links up with the wider origin legend for the Celtic peoples of the British Isles as the descendants of the lost tribe of Dan.

In its 'Irish period', the stone acquired the name *Lia Fail*, or stone of destiny, and is said to have been sited at Tara, the holy hill on which Ireland's high kings were crowned. A piece of it was apparently broken off and taken to the Irish colony of Dál Riata in Argyllshire, possibly even by Columba who according to some stories used it as his pillow or his altar. After residing at Iona for a time, and possibly being used at Dunadd for the crowning of Dál Riatan kings, it was taken to Dunstaffnage Castle near Oban, the seat and burial place of later Dál Riatan kings. Around 840 it was moved to Scone in Perthshire, the capital of the new united kingdom of Picts and Scots established by Kenneth MacAlpin. Kings of Scotland were thereafter enthroned sitting on the stone at Scone, the last to do so before Edward's removal of the stone to London being John Balliol in 1292. Edward seized the stone as part of his bid to annex the Scottish crown to that of England, reckoning that its possession made him the legal king of Scotland and that any subsequently elected Scottish king would be a usurper and not properly crowned. Although they no longer had the stone to sit on, nearly all subsequent kings of Scotland continued to be crowned at Scone.

It is in fact highly dubious whether the stone which currently resides in Edinburgh Castle is the one which MacAlpin brought to Scone, let alone whether it originally came from the Holy Land. The sandstone of which it is made is of a type relatively common in the areas around both Scone and Dunstaffnage but unknown in the vicinity of Tara or in the Middle East. This is an area, however, where hard facts are less important than legend and myth. The Stone of Destiny symbolises the sacred character and history of monarchy in the British Isles and illustrates the considerable efforts which have been made to connect it with Old Testament kingship and biblical narratives. For British Israelites, it is an important part of the evidence showing a direct descent of the British royal house from the throne of David. Symbolically and spiritually, the stone links the crowns of Ireland, Scotland and England. In the words of Arthur Stanley, Dean of Westminster from 1863 to 1881, it 'carries back our thoughts to races and customs now almost extinct, a link which unites the throne of England to the traditions of Tara and Iona, and connects the charm of our complex civilization with the forces of our mother earth – the sticks and stones of savage nature.'[3]

The Anointing

In every coronation of which a record survives, the anointing of the monarch has been preceded by the singing of the great ninth-century Latin hymn, *Veni, Creator Spiritus*, to its original plainsong tune. Since James II's coronation it has been sung in John Cousin's English translation which begins 'Come, Holy Ghost, our souls inspire'. This hymn, which is regularly used at the election of popes, the consecration of bishops in both the Roman Catholic and Anglican churches and the ordination of priests and ministers in a large number of different denominations, specifically refers to the anointing work of the Holy Spirit with its 'blessed unction from above'.

For the anointing a canopy made of silk or cloth of gold is held over the monarch, traditionally by four Knights of the Garter. The Dean of Westminster takes from the altar the *ampulla,* a solid gold jug fashioned in the form of an eagle containing the holy oil, made up of sesame and olive oil perfumed with rose petals and jasmine and seasoned with musk, civet and ambergris, and pours some into the spoon which he hands to the Archbishop. The spoon, which is made of silver, is the only item of the coronation regalia which dates back before the mid-seventeenth century. Everything else was destroyed following Charles I's execution and the inauguration of the Commonwealth and Protectorate in 1649 on the orders of Oliver Cromwell with the result that all the rest of the regalia now in use were first made for the coronation of Charles II in 1661.

The actual anointing takes place with the monarch hidden from public view and seated on King Edward's chair while the choir sing the anthem 'Zadok the priest and Nathan the prophet', vividly recalling Solomon's consecration. The Archbishop also makes direct reference to Solomon's anointing as he pours a small quantity of oil on to the palms of both hands, the breast and head, making the sign of the cross at each stage.

Investing with Royal and Priestly Robes

The anointing over, the canopy is borne away by the Knights of the Garter and the monarch is vested in the *colobium sindonis*, *supertunica*, girdle and stole royal. These garments are based on ecclesiastical vestments and are designed to emphasize the sacerdotal and episcopal character of monarchy. The *colobium sindonis* is to all intents and purposes a priest's alb or surplice or bishop's rochet. A sleeveless garment made of white linen with a lace border, it is open at the side, gathered in at the waist and cut low at the neck. Over it is put the *supertunica,* identical to a priest's dalmatic, a close-fitting long coat fashioned in rich silk cloth of gold. A girdle of the same material which is put round the waist has a gold buckle and hangers on which to suspend the sword with which the monarch is girded. The stole placed over the shoulders is a band of cloth of gold heavily embroidered with gold and silver thread with a square panel at either end on which the red cross of St George is embroidered on a silver background.

Presentation of spurs and sword

A pair of solid gold spurs, with straps of crimson velvet embroidered with gold, have traditionally been brought to the sovereign at this point. Known as St George's spurs, they symbolize chivalry and knightly virtue, as described in the once popular children's hymn 'When a knight won his spurs in the stories of old/He was gentle and brave, he was gallant and bold'. Next comes the presentation of the monarch's sword, the symbolism of which is conveyed in the Archbishop's accompanying prayer from the 1953 coronation:

> With this Sword do justice, stop the growth of iniquity, protect the Holy Church of God, help and defend widows and orphans, restore the things that are gone into decay, maintain the things that are restored, punish and reform what is amiss, and confirm what is in good order.[4]

Traditionally five swords are carried and used in coronations. The double-handed Sword of State is the largest and there are also the swords of spiritual and temporal justice and the sword of mercy, also known as the Curtana. The monarch is presented with the most elaborate of the five, the jewelled state sword made for the coronation of George IV. In the case of a king, this sword is girded, while queens, including Victoria and Elizabeth II, have held it in their hands. In both cases, it is then offered in its scabbard on the altar, after which it is traditionally redeemed for the sum of 100 shillings by a peer who draws it from its scabbard and carries it naked with the point upwards for the rest of the service.

Investiture with the Armills and Imperial Mantle

Next a pair of bracelets, known as armills, are traditionally put on the monarch's wrists by the Archbishop with the words:

> Receive the bracelets of sincerity and wisdom, both for tokens of the Lord's protection embracing you on every side; and also for

symbols and pledges of that bond which unites you with your Peoples: to the end that you may be strengthened in all your works and defended against your enemies both bodily and ghostly.[5]

The investiture continues with the monarch being vested in the imperial mantle or *pallium regale*, a rich cloth of gold cope similar to those worn by bishops and embroidered with the national emblems of rose, shamrock and thistle as well as silver eagles, gold coronets and *fleurs-de-lys*, as the Archbishop says, 'the Lord clothe you with the robe of righteousness, and with the garments of salvation'.[6]

Investiture with the Orb, Ring, Sceptre and Rod

The orb, which has customarily been put into the monarch's right hand, is the oldest emblem of Christian sovereignty, used by later Roman Emperors and Anglo-Saxon kings. A ball of gold surmounted by a large cross thickly studded with diamonds and set in an amethyst base, it acts as a reminder, in the Archbishop's words, 'that the whole world is subject to the Power and Empire of Christ'.[7] Its first appearances in Britain are on a seal of Edward the Confessor in use between 1053 and 1065 and in a depiction of the crowning of King Harold in the Bayeux Tapestry, in both cases being held in the king's left hand. The orb has not always been used in English coronations: neither Henry VII or Henry VIII were invested with one. The complex planning of Charles III's coronation is code-named 'Operation Golden Orb', suggesting that this particular 'prop' will feature on 6 May 2023.

The ring, in Latin *annulus*, which is next traditionally placed on the fourth finger of the right hand has often been specifically made to fit the new sovereign, although Elizabeth II used an existing one inlaid with a ruby and engraved with St George's cross. Another item among the royal regalia with obvious episcopal connotations, it is presented to symbolise the marriage of monarch and country and was known in medieval times as 'the wedding ring of England'. Elizabeth I, who wore her coronation ring throughout her reign, told Mary Queen of Scots' ambassador in 1561: 'I am already married to the realm of England when I was crowned with this ring which I wear continuously in token thereof'.[8]

The final pieces of regalia with which a monarch is traditionally invested before being crowned are known in Latin as the *sceptrus* and the *baculus*. These may originally have derived from the rod and staff mentioned in Psalm 23 and in the coronation service they are referred to as the royal sceptre and rod. The solid gold sceptre has since 1910 contained the largest clear cut diamond in the world, part of the massive Cullinan diamond found in the Transvaal in 1905. It is surmounted by a cross, which stands for kingly power and justice. The longer rod, also made of solid gold, is surmounted by a dove, signifying equity and mercy. They provide a link to pre-Christian inauguration rites when monarchs were invested with a rod which was white to represent truth and purity and straight to symbolise justice and uprightness. Before receiving the sceptre and rod, the monarch is presented with a specially made glove which is then worn on the right hand. Queen Elizabeth II's glove was made of white kid leather, embroidered with a raised 'E II R' in gold, and a red velvet queenly crown above, the gauntlet cuff arrayed with an intricate design of roses, acorns and shamrocks.

Crowning

The crowning, like the various investitures which precede it, takes places with the monarch sitting on King Edward's Chair. The crown used in recent coronations is known as St Edward's crown but is in fact a copy made for Charles II's coronation of the original used for crowning medieval monarchs. Considered a holy relic, it was kept in Westminster Abbey until it was broken up in 1649 on the orders of the Long Parliament. The replica St Edward's Crown was not used after 1689 until King George V revived the tradition of wearing it in 1911. Weighing over 4½ lbs., its rim is set with gems and there are two gold arches symbolizing sovereignty. Where they meet there is a gold orb surmounted by a jewelled cross. This crown is only used at coronations. As it is placed by the Archbishop on the monarch's head, it is traditional for all those gathered in the Abbey to make loud and repeated shouts of 'God save the King/Queen', trumpets to sound, and a signal given for the firing of guns at the Tower of London. The acclamation having ceased, the Archbishop says:

> God crown you with a crown of glory and righteousness, that having a right faith and manifold fruit of good works, you may obtain the crown of an everlasting kingdom by the gift of him whose kingdom endureth for ever.[9]

Benediction, enthroning and homage

The monarch, having now 'received all the ensigns of royalty', is blessed by the Archbishop using words based on the blessing given by Archbishop William

Sancroft when he crowned James II in 1685. This was the Benediction given to Elizabeth II:

> The Lord give you faithful Parliaments and quiet Realms; sure defence against all enemies; fruitful lands and a prosperous industry; wise counsellors and upright magistrates; leaders of integrity in learning and labour; a devout, learned, and useful clergy; honest, peaceable, and dutiful citizens. May wisdom and knowledge be the stability of your times, and the fear of the Lord your treasure'.[10]

A second benediction is then delivered to the congregation.

For the enthroning the monarch is traditionally 'lifted up by the archbishops, bishops and other peers of the kingdom' from King Edward's Chair to the throne set up in the theatre, echoing the old custom whereby a new king was lifted on to a shield by his followers and exhibited to the people. In recent coronations monarchs have made their own way to the throne. The homage which has traditionally followed, in which princes and peers kneel before the throne and declare that they would be faithful and true, followed by general acclamation, the beating of drums and sounding of trumpets, seems unlikely to be part of King Charles III's coronation. The report on 'The Coronation of Charles III' published by the Constitution Unit, University College London, in October 2022 points out that 'it is not part of the religious rite but a hangover from the feudal constitution' and recommends that it be dropped.[11]

Anointing and coronation of the Queen Consort

If usual practice is followed, the Queen Consort will be anointed, crowned and invested with a ring, a sceptre and an ivory rod. This last happened in the 1937 coronation of King George VI and Queen Elizabeth.

Communion

There now follows the communion service, celebrated according to the Book of Common Prayer. The monarch and consort take off their crowns, give up their sceptres and rods and kneel before the altar. The king offers to the Archbishop first bread and wine, brought from St Edward's Chapel, and then an oblation or offering of a pall or altar-cloth and an ingot of gold weighing a pound contained in an embroidered velvet bag. This oblation is described in the *Liber Regalis* as being made in direct imitation of the actions of the priest-king Melchizedek. Traditionally, only the King and Queen, the Archbishop of Canterbury and the Dean of Westminster receive communion.

The Recess

At the end of the service the choir sing the *Te Deum Laudamus* and the King and Queen process to St Edward's Chapel where the King, in a fourth and final change of garment, is divested of the imperial mantle, or *pallium*, and arrayed in a robe of purple velvet. Purple was the colour associated with Roman emperors and had by the fourth century come to have sacramental and mystical significance. St Edward's Crown is exchanged for the Imperial

State Crown, made for Queen Victoria in 1838 and used for the state opening of parliament. It contains the Black Prince's ruby, part of the Cullinan diamond, a sapphire reputedly taken from Edward the Confessor's ring and four large drop pearls which reputedly belonged to Elizabeth I. For their final procession through the Abbey, both King and Queen wear crowns, he holds in his right hand the Sceptre with the Cross and in his left hand the Orb and she carries her Sceptre and Ivory Rod.

Mumbo jumbo or imaginative symbolism?

On the face of it, the traditional coronation service seems like a mixture of medieval mumbo jumbo and make-believe. Can there really be any place in the inauguration of a twenty-first-century head of state for spurs and bracelets, swords and imperial mantles, not to mention a cracked piece of sandstone with an unbelievable back story? Some of the 'props' and pieces of regalia used in previous ceremonies and described in this chapter may not feature in Charles III's coronation. Press reports have suggested that 'a number of rituals, including the presentation of gold ingots, will be removed'.[12] Whether this refers to the presentation of spurs, the investiture with armills, or the oblation of a gold ingot traditionally made in the communion service, or possibly all three, is not clear. Rowan Williams, who was involved in discussions about the shape of the coronation during his time as Archbishop of Canterbury, is quoted by Catherine Pepinster in her book *Defender of the Faith: The British Monarchy, Religion and the Next Coronation* as saying, 'the Gilbert and Sullivan aspects will go'.[13] He is probably thinking here of serried ranks of peers doffing their coronets, as they might in *Iolanthe*, rather than the allusions to medieval chivalry and Tudor valour that one might find in *Princess Ida* or *The Yeomen of the Guard* – I certainly hope so.

Could it in fact be the case that the mumbo-jumbo and make-believe of the traditional coronation strike a distinct contemporary chord and speak with uncanny relevance to our present situation? We live at a time when Dungeons and Dragons, the *Game of Thrones*, the wizardry of Hogwarts and the *Lord of the Rings* have enormous appeal and when the popular imagination is fed and touched by stories of chivalry, knightly derring-do and mystical magic not so very different from those which inspired the original construction of the coronation service so many centuries ago. We also live in a time of considerable uncertainty and acute anxiety. I find myself in strong agreement with the sentiments expressed by Cosmo Gordon Lang before he presided as Archbishop of Canterbury over the coronation of George VI, at which he was described by *Time* magazine as 'the most important person there, a hawk-nosed old gentleman with a cream-&-gold cope':

> Some persons may ask – many more may think – 'are not all these ancient rites and ceremonies quite out of place in this modern world?' The question surely argues a singular lack of imagination - of that faculty which visualises the significance of history. It is no mere paradox to say that the very merit and meaning of these rites is precisely that they are in a sense 'out of date'. How could the wonderful stability and continuity of the national history be more impressively shown? But in another sense they are most truly - to use the common phrase – 'up to date'. Consider the world around us -

ancient empires and monarchies vanished, new dictatorships created, everywhere restlessness and uncertainty about the future. In the midst our king is to be crowned with the same rights as those with which his predecessors have been crowned for more than a thousand years.

Moreover, although the forms are old, the spirit embodied in them and expressed in the words attached to them is never old and may ever be renewed. The spirit is the solemn recognition of the sacred character alike of royalty and loyalty – that 'the powers that be are ordained of God', that the ultimate source and sanction of all true civil rule and obedience is the Will and Purpose of God, that behind the things that are seen and temporal are the things that are unseen and eternal.[14]

Chapter 8

REFLECTIONS ON CORONATIONS

Coronations are occasions for reflecting on and affirming the sacred meaning of monarchy. I trust this will be the case with the coronation of King Charles III and Queen Camilla. This chapter gathers together some reflections prompted by previous coronations, both from Christian leaders and more secularly minded commentators. I begin with words from a famous diarist which point to their sheer splendour and significance and the extent to which they linger in the mind and change perspectives. After attending the English coronation of Charles II in 1661, Samuel Pepys wrote:

> Now after all this, I can say that, besides the pleasure of the sight of these glorious things, I may now shut my eyes against any other objects, or for the future trouble myself to see things of state and show, as being sure never to see the like again in this world.[1]

The evangelical politician and philanthropist Lord Ashley, later the Earl of Shaftesbury, was similarly moved by Queen Victoria's coronation, feeling its spiritual power and refuting those who dismissed it as 'an idle pageant':

An idle pageant, forsooth! As idle as the Coronation of King Solomon, or the dedication of his Temple. The service itself refutes the notion; so solemn, so deeply religious, so humbling, and yet so sublime! Every word of it is invaluable; throughout the Church is everything, secular greatness nothing. She declares, in the name and by the authority of God, and almost enforces, as a condition preliminary to the benediction, all that can make Princes wise to temporal and eternal glory.[2]

Looking ahead to the coronation that never was, of Edward VIII in 1936, Alfred Blunt, Bishop of Bradford, emphasized the significance and implications of the ceremony for the population at large:

Whatever it may mean to the individual who is crowned, to the people as a whole it means their dedication of the English monarchy to the care of God, in whose rule and governance are the hearts of kings.

Not only as important as but far more important than the King's personal feelings are to his Coronation, is the feeling with which we – the people of England – view it. Our part of the ceremony is to fill it with reality, by the sincerity of our belief in the power of God to over-rule for good our national history, and by the sincerity with which we commend the King and nation to his Providence.

Are we going to be merely spectators or listeners-in as at any other interesting function, with a sort of passive curiosity? Or are we in some sense going to consecrate ourselves to the service of God and the welfare of mankind?[3]

This challenging statement about the extent to which coronations require popular 'buy-in', to use the popular contemporary term, is unusual although it chimes in with the idea of the three way covenant between God, monarch and people. More common have been reflections on the consecration and dedication of the one being anointed and crowned, such as those expressed in *The Times* leader on the day of George VI's coronation in 1937:

> Nothing is heard nowadays of the 'divine right'; and not since the last of the Stewarts, Queen Anne, has any sovereign of England been credited with the magical 'touch' for the cure of the 'King's Evil'. Yet, seeing the king thus exalted at this most solemn moment above common humanity, the mind's eye may catch, beyond all the pomp, another vision. It is a vision to hush the enthusiasm, but only in order to deepen the feeling of loyalty and turn good will into prayer. The king is on his way to be enthroned, indeed, and acclaimed. The trumpets will sound and the people will cry out 'God save King George!'. But he is on his way also to be consecrated – to be dedicated. Once that is done, he is no longer an ordinary man. He is a man dedicated.

The leader went on to discuss the primal pagan idea of the ritual sacrifice of the king.

> In the modern world, the king is dedicated to a harder sacrifice. Day in and day out, for his people he must live... The more closely the burden of kingship is looked at, the more impossible does it seem that any man should bear it unless he

were sustained and fortified and inspired by the spiritual power conferred on him in Westminster Abbey today.[4]

For its leader on Coronation Day 1953 *The Times* returned to the primal image of the monarch as the incarnation of the people, a phrase which had been used by Archbishop William Temple in connection with the coronation of George V, while also reiterating the point made by Bishop Blunt about the participation of the entire population:

> Today's sublime ceremonial is in form, and in common view, a dedication of the state to God's service through the prayers and benedictions of the Church. That is a noble conception, and of itself makes every man and woman in the land a partaker in the mystery of the Queen's anointing. But also the Queen stands for the soul as well as the body of the Commonwealth. In her is incarnate on her Coronation day the whole of society, of which the state is no more than a political manifestation. She represents the life of her people ... as men and women, and not in their limited capacity as Lords and Commons and electors. It is the glory of the social monarchy that it sets the human above the institutional.[5]

There is a danger in over-spiritualising the coronation and using somewhat hyperbolic language about its significance. On the day of Queen Elizabeth II's coronation in 1953 Geoffrey Fisher, as Archbishop of Canterbury, solemnly announced that England had been brought closer to the kingdom of heaven and another senior cleric declared that it was 'a miracle that might save civilisation'. The prominent humanist and socialist journalist, Kingsley Martin, was justified in observing that 'extravagant views of monarchy are usually expressed at coronations.'[6] Other secularist commentators criticized the 1953 coronation for being altogether too religious in tone. In his trenchant attack on the monarchy in general, and the Queen in particular, for being totally out of touch, published in 1958, John Grigg, newly ennobled as Lord Altrincham, complained that 'the Coronation had emphasized the priestly aspect of her office and in the ensuing period she had continued to appear more sacerdotal than secular'.[7]

In general, however, journalists and authors writing about the last coronation acknowledged and welcomed its sacred character. For the former *Times* religious affairs correspondent and *Daily Telegraph* and *Tablet* columnist, Clifford Longley,

> The Coronation of our Queen was an act of God performed by human hands, and the assembly held its breath at the mystery and wonder of it. It was one of the central acts of statehood, the moment whereby all temporal authority in the realm flowing from the king was legitimised and sanctified. This is the doctrine of Christian kingship.[8]

Perhaps more surprisingly the somewhat cynical and world-weary Jeremy Paxman found himself in his 2006 book *On Royalty* acknowledging and affirming the religious character of the coronation and its testimony to the essentially sacred nature of monarchy:

The ceremony's function is to knit together the elements of acclamation with the fact that the monarch is already king or queen simply because his or her predecessor has died. For hundreds of years in Britain these potentially contradictory elements have been reconciled by a ritual which is conspicuously and overwhelmingly religious.... It is a Christian spectacular, with the elders of the church pressing in around the new king or queen, and the state allowed access only through the mediation of the clergy... The echoes of the Christ story are not merely implied but explicit, which is why the only appropriate setting for the ritual is a religious one. Without it, the coronation would be a meaningless piece of civic theatre.

Cold reasoning says that there is no reason why a king should not assume office in a ceremony shorn of religious ritual and anachronistic flummery. An impresario who attempted to stage such an event for a king would find himself having to address some very awkward questions. In wealthy western societies the idea of the sacred has been steadily impoverished ever since the Industrial Revolution. Monarchy is almost the last institution in the land to which any mystique attaches. Indeed, the mystique is the most powerful guarantor of its survival. To remove the element of magic from the ritual of enthronement might well leave the institution so exposed that it would wither and die.[9]

Paxman went on to reflect that 'monarchs stand for something beyond themselves, and in that sense are less political creatures than religious ones' and that 'there is certainly an argument for saying that royalty can be properly understood only in religious terms'.[10]

The most profound and in some ways surprising reflection on this topic comes in an academic article about the meaning of the last coronation by two sociologists, Edward Shils and Michael Young, in an article in the *Sociological Review* in 1953. For them, 'the coronation was the ceremonial occasion for the affirmation of the moral values by which the society lives. It was an act of national communion and an intensive contact with the sacred.'[11] Their argument was based in part on their observation of the coronation's impact on 'ordinary' people. They noted that it was frequently spoken of as an 'inspiration' and a 're-dedication of the nation'. The ceremony had 'touched the sense of the sacred' in people, heightening a sense of solidarity in both families and communities. They pointed to examples of reconciliation between long-feuding neighbours and family members brought about by the shared experience of watching the ceremony together on television and noted that the crowds lining the streets of London on Coronation Day were not idle curiosity seekers but 'looking for contact with something which is connected with the sacred'.

Shils, Professor of Sociology at the University of Chicago, and Young, a former research secretary of the Labour Party, argued that Elizabeth II's coronation had enabled people to affirm moral values, notably 'generosity, charity, loyalty, justice in the distribution of opportunities and rewards, reasonable respect for authority, the dignity of the individual and his right to freedom'.[12] The sacred properties and charisma of the crown strengthened the moral consensus prevailing in Britain.

> The monarchy is the one pervasive institution, standing above all others, which plays a part in a vital way comparable to the function of the medieval church ... the function of integrating diverse elements into a whole by protecting and defining their autonomy.[13]

What is remarkable about these statements is that they came not from churchmen or monarchists but left-leaning sociologists who were particularly struck by the morally cohesive effect produced by the actual form of the coronation ceremony.

> The Coronation Service itself is a series of ritual affirmations of the moral values necessary to a well-governed and good society. The key to the Coronation Service is the Queen's promise to abide by the moral standards of society.[14]

In addition to the oath which Shils and Young singled out as being especially important in this regard, the act of anointing and the investiture with the bracelets of sincerity and wisdom, the orb and the sword were also identified as being not just symbolic but transformative in bringing Queen and people 'into a great nation-wide communion'.[15] 'The Coronation', they concluded, 'provided at one time and for practically the entire society such an intensive contact with the sacred that we believe we are justified in interpreting it as we have done in this essay, as a great act of national communion.'[16]

Will future sociologists and commentators write

in similar terms about the 2023 coronation? We are a much more fractured, secular and diverse society now than we were 70 years ago. Yet perhaps for that very reason the coronation of Charles III may speak to and partially answer the yearning for unity, healing and spirituality which so many manifestly feel. Shils and Young noted that the 1953 coronation service, stage managed by the Church of England, 'served the vague religiosity of the British people'.[17] That vague religiosity is still there, latent, barely articulated, but ready to be inspired and touched. The late Queen's death undoubtedly released it. Maybe so, too, will her son's coronation.

PART 4
The Monarch's Religious Rules and Responsibilities

Being monarch of the United Kingdom officially involves governing the Church of England and defending the Faith. Solemn oaths taken at accession and coronation commit the sovereign to protecting Protestantism and preserving the established churches. The next four chapters explore these roles and responsibilities, look at the way that they are being re-interpreted in an increasingly multifaith and secular country and provide a guide to the regular royal religious engagements through the year.

Chapter 9

PROTECTOR OF PROTESTANTISM

The close relationship between the British monarchy and Protestant Christianity has already been explored in Chapter 5. It could, indeed, be said that the maintenance and promotion of Protestantism in the United Kingdom remains the monarch's clearest and most conspicuous religious duty, expressed in binding oaths taken at accession and in the coronation. There is also a legal bar on a Roman Catholic coming to the throne. Archaic and anachronistic as it may seem in an overwhelmingly secular country where only a tiny handful of people consciously identify as Protestants and where there are almost certainly more Roman Catholics than Anglicans in church on a Sunday morning, the monarchy remains almost the last champion of proudly and defiantly Protestant Britain.

The laws establishing the monarchy's role as protector of Protestantism date from the aftermath of the 1688-9 Glorious Revolution although its origins go back to the later sixteenth century and the concept of the godly prince as the key agent in promoting Reformed religion in his or her territory. Its roots can, indeed, be traced back further to the tussle between mediaeval monarchs and the papacy, seen as an interfering foreign power, compounded by the fact that England's traditional rivals, notably Spain and France, were staunchly Catholic countries.

A widespread popular and visceral anti-Catholicism was reinforced by a Brexit-like Little Englander xenophobia and distrust of foreigners, although fellow Protestants like the Dutch and Germans were excluded from this hostility and indeed came to supply occupants of the United Kingdom throne from William of Orange onwards. In both the popular and official mind, Catholicism became associated with tyranny, obscurantism, priestcraft and effeminacy in contrast to the stout, manly Anglo-Saxon (and Scottish) virtues of freedom, liberty of conscience and self-reliance. Anti-Catholicism was further fuelled by the ramifications of what became known as the Irish question, which increasingly impinged on mainland British politics and society and made Ulster Protestants the most loyal monarchists of any part of the UK.

It was the peculiar circumstances of 1688-9 that gave the Crown its central role as protector of the Protestant religion. The English and Scottish parliaments deposed James II and VII primarily because he was a Roman Catholic and had produced a Roman Catholic male heir. They invited the staunchly Calvinist William, Prince of Orange and Stadtholder of Holland, Zeeland, Utrecht, Guelders, and Overijssel in the Dutch Republic and his wife Mary, James's daughter, to be King and Queen of England, Ireland, and Scotland.

1688 Bill of Rights and Coronation Oaths Act

Two key pieces of legislation passed by the English Parliament in 1688 required the new monarchs to make a very clear commitment to Protestantism. The first, part of the Bill of Rights, required 'every King and Queen of this Realm who at any time hereafter shall come to and succeed in the Imperial Crown of this Kingdom' to make the following declaration either at their first meeting with Parliament or at their coronation:

> I do solemnly, in the presence of God, profess, testify, and declare, that I do believe that in the sacrament of the Lord's Supper, there is not any transubstantiation of the elements of bread and wine into the body and blood of Christ, at or after the consecration thereof by any person whatsoever. 2ndly, That the invocation or adoration of the Virgin Mary, or any other saint, and the sacrifice of the mass, as they are now used in the church of Rome, are superstitious and idolatrous.

This declaration had first appeared in an Act of 1678 'for the more effectual Preserving the King's Person and Government by disabling Papists from sitting in either House of Parliament' which required it to be taken by all peers and members of the House of Commons before they could sit in Parliament and also by civil and military officials. The Bill of Rights extended it to the monarch. Following the repeal of the Test Acts with the coming of Catholic emancipation in 1829, only the monarch was required to continue to make the declaration.

The second piece of legislation, the Coronation Oaths Act, changed the third oath taken by monarchs at their coronation relating to the protection of church and clergy. This had already been altered in the light of the Reformation. At his English coronation in 1603, James I had sworn to maintain not just 'the laws of God' but also 'the true profession of the Gospel established in this kingdom', a format that was kept for all subsequent Stuart coronations. William III was additionally required to maintain 'the Protestant Reformed Religion Established by Law', a commitment that has remained in the third coronation oath ever since.

The Scottish Claim of Right and Scottish Oath

The Scottish equivalent of the English Bill of Rights, the 1689 Claim of Rights, which offered the Crown to William and Mary, laid down that 'no papist can be king or queen of this realm'. The Scottish Convention, a gathering of the Estates which formally became the Scottish Parliament in late 1689, devised its own oath for the new monarchs, based on one used at the Scottish coronation of James VI. It required them to swear to uphold and 'maintain the true religion of Jesus Christ, the preaching of his holy word and due right administration of the sacraments now received and preached within the realm of Scotland' and to 'root out all heretics and enemies to the true worship of God that shall be convicted by the true Kirk of God'.[1]

William was uneasy about the reference to rooting out heretics as he felt that it made him a 'persecutor' which he did not see as part of his royal duties. Having been assured that 'no man was to be persecuted for his private opinion', he duly agreed to take the oath at a meeting with delegates from the Scottish Convention in the Banqueting House in Whitehall. The Scottish oath was also taken by Queen Anne when she succeeded to the throne in 1702.

1701 Act of Settlement and 1707 Act of Union

With neither William and Mary, nor Anne, whose sole surviving child, the Duke of Gloucester, died aged 11 in 1700, producing any heirs, there was considerable concern that James's Catholic son, also called James and later known as 'the Old Pretender', would claim the throne. In order to ensure a Protestant succession, the English Parliament enacted the 1701 Act of Settlement which provided that, failing the issue of Anne and of William III by any future marriage, the Crown of England and Ireland would go to Sophia, Electress of Hanover, grand-daughter of James VI and I, and her Protestant descendants. The Act laid down in the clearest possible terms:

> That all and every person and persons that should be reconciled to, or should hold Communion with the See or Church of Rome, or should profess the Popish Religion, or marry a Papist, should be excluded, and are by that Act made for ever incapable to inherit, possess or enjoy the Crown and Government of this Realm.

In their determination to prevent a Roman Catholic from succeeding to the throne those responsible for framing this Act passed over more than fifty close blood relations of Anne in order to arrive at the acceptably Protestant figure of Sophia, Electress of Hanover and her heirs. In the event, it was Sophie's son, George, Elector of Hanover, who succeeded to the throne of England, Ireland and Scotland in 1714.

The Scottish Parliament had not been consulted about the Act of Settlement and had passed an Act of Security in 1703 reserving Scotland's right to make its own choice with regard to the succession. There were fears on the English side that on Anne's death, the Scots might favour the accession of her exiled Roman Catholic half-brother, James Edward Stuart, if they were not locked into a parliamentary union. The Treaty of Union with Scotland in 1707 brought Scotland into line with England and confirmed the Protestant succession through Sophia and her heirs. It incorporated into United Kingdom legislation one of the last acts passed by the pre-Union Parliament of Scotland, 'An Act for Securing the Protestant Religion and Presbyterian Church Government', known in shortened form as the Protestant Religion and Presbyterian Church Act 1707, drawn up to ensure that the status of the Church of Scotland would not be affected by the Union with England.

The 1707 Act of Union between England and Scotland, which gave full legislative effect to the Treaty of Union, added to the coronation oath a promise to 'maintain and preserve inviolably the settlement of the Church of England and the doctrine, worship, discipline, and government thereof' and also required that each new monarch should swear on accession to maintain the Protestant religion and Presbyterian government of the Church of Scotland in accordance with the terms of the Protestant Religion and Presbyterian Church Act. At the Accession Council held on 10 September 2022 when he was formally declared king, Charles III duly took what has become known as 'the Scottish oath':

I, Charles the Third, by the Grace of God of the United Kingdom of Great Britain and Northern Ireland and of My other Realms and Territories, King, Defender of the Faith, do faithfully promise and swear that I shall inviolably maintain and preserve the Settlement of the true Protestant Religion as established by the Laws made in Scotland in prosecution of the Claim of Right.

The eighteenth century

In her book, *Britons: Forging the Nation*, Linda Colley demonstrated the extent to which, in the absence of any ethnic sense of nationhood, Protestantism, or perhaps more precisely anti-Catholicism, became the great uniting force in the creation of the new United Kingdom of the English, Welsh and Scots in the eighteenth century. The monarchy was a key focus of this Protestant national identity, much of which was achieved through the assiduous application of what we would now call spin and public relations. National days of commemoration were promoted to remind people of key events in the development of the Protestant monarchy – 30 January commemorated the execution of Charles I; 29 May the restoration of monarchy in 1660; 1 August the accession of the Hanoverians in 1714; and 5 November was the occasion for a double celebration of both the foiling of the Catholic-inspired Gunpowder Plot against James I and the landing of William of Orange in 1688.

The Protestantism of the British monarchy was regularly celebrated by clergy. Preaching at the coronation of George I, the Bishop of Oxford, William Talbot, tactfully ignoring the fact that the new king had left his wife behind in Germany and brought two of his mistresses, known respectively as the elephant and the maypole, with him to London, hailed him as a new David and, in an allusion to the exiled Young Pretender, rejoiced that the British throne had been spared 'one educated in the Maxims of French Tyranny and the Principles of Popish Superstition'.[2]

Two Hanoverian monarchs made personal interventions in fulfilment of what they saw as their solemn duty to protect Protestantism. George III forced the resignation of his Prime Minister in 1801 because he regarded William Pitt's proposals for Roman Catholic emancipation in Ireland as contravening his coronation oath. He opposed Catholic emancipation in the rest of the United Kingdom on the same grounds. George IV did all he could to oppose the efforts of his Prime Minister, the Duke of Wellington, and Home Secretary, Robert Peel, to secure Catholic emancipation in 1828 in an attempt to pacify increasing tension in Ireland. In a six-hour discussion with leading members of the Cabinet the evening before the Catholic Relief Bill was due to be put before Parliament, he threatened to abdicate if he had to give royal assent to a measure which he felt to be contrary to the solemn and sacred oath he had taken at his coronation. His ministers held their ground and eventually at a late-night dinner with his private secretary and other advisers, he was persuaded to agree to the proposed legislation. He sent Wellington a note advising of his last-minute surrender, adding 'God knows what pain it costs me to write these words'.[3]

Victoria

Queen Victoria's promotion of Protestantism derived as much from the nature of her own faith and ecclesiastical preferences as from the coronation oaths and accession declarations she had made. Under the twin influences of her mother's evangelicalism and her beloved husband's Lutheranism, her Christianity had a distinctly Protestant hue. She had a strong preference for plain 'low church' worship and a pronounced antipathy towards the High Church ritualistic tendency in the Church of England. Whatever their persuasion, clergy preaching before her were required to wear a simple black gown, and private services in her presence were conducted without the aid of vestments, candles, processions or other ornamental accessories. A journalist observed in 1888 'It is no secret that, with her Lutheran sympathies, she feels more at home among Presbyterian than Episcopal surroundings. She is a very staunch Protestant and heartily dislikes all forms of ritualism and sacerdotal pretension'.[4] The queen herself made clear the main reason for her partiality to the established church north of the border: 'Thank God, the Scotch Church is a stronghold of Protestantism, most precious in these realms.'[5]

Victoria was keen to push the Church of England in a more Protestant direction. In 1873 she sent a series of letters to Arthur Stanley, the Dean of Westminster, lamenting the fact that the Church of England had not been 'reformed as every other Protestant Church has been ... We are in fact in form NOT Protestants though we are in doctrine.' She went on to express her own preference 'for the sweeping Reformation of the English Church'. If this was not possible, then at least 'the Archbishop should have the power given to him, by Parliament, to stop these ritualistic practices, dressings, bowings, etc.'[6] The Public Worship Regulation Act, passed by Parliament the following year, and designed to curb 'Popish' and ritualistic practices in the Church of England, was widely seen as in part a product of her direct intervention and was one of the last measures resulting from a proactive use of the royal prerogative. It led to five Anglican clergymen being imprisoned for such offences as lighting eucharistic candles, wearing unlawful vestments, kneeling during the prayer of consecration, mixing water and communion wine, making the sign of the Cross towards the congregation during the Holy Communion service and adoration of the Blessed Sacrament.

1910 Accession Declaration Act

The vehemently anti-Catholic declaration of personal belief required by the 1688 Bill of Rights was made without apparent demur by every British monarch throughout the eighteenth and nineteenth centuries. At his accession in 1901, however, Edward VII protested at its 'crude language' which he considered an insult to his Roman Catholic subjects. With the approval of the Cabinet, he asked for it to be changed but nothing was done, much to his annoyance. Edward, who according to some sources himself made a death-bed conversion to Catholicism, signalled his unease by making the declaration in a low monotone. His successor George V refused to open Parliament until a less insulting form of words was substituted. Herbert Asquith, the Prime Minister, felt that the whole declaration could be scrapped but influential voices in the Church of England and the Free Churches insisted that it be kept. The Accession Declaration Act of 1910 substituted a considerably modified declaration, drawn up by the Archbishop of Canterbury, Randall Davidson, which has been used ever since:

> I do solemnly and sincerely in the presence of God profess, testify and declare that I am a faithful Protestant and that I will according to the true intent of the enactments which secure the Protestant succession to the Throne of my Realm, uphold and maintain the said enactment to the best of my powers according to the law.

Michael Bloch claims that Edward VIII wished to dispense with the Protestant declaration altogether but because of his abdication, the matter never came to the test.[7] The declaration was made by Queen Elizabeth II in the form above when she opened the first Parliament of her reign in November 1952.

Succession to the throne

At a meeting in Perth, Australia, in 2011 the heads of government of the 16 Commonwealth countries of which the Queen was head agreed to repeal the clause in the 1701 Act of Settlement which barred anyone married to a Roman Catholic from succession to the throne. The ensuing Succession to the Crown Act, which came into effect in 2013, ended a somewhat anomalous aspect of the British constitution which has long baffled foreigners and outraged human rights campaigners and which allowed the monarch to be married to a Muslim, a Moonie or a militant atheist but not to a Roman Catholic.

It remains impossible for a Catholic to occupy the British throne and there is a further stipulation that the monarch must be a member of the Church of England (see page 178). The United Kingdom is not the only country to impose restrictions on the religion of its sovereign. The constitutions of Norway, Sweden and Denmark require that the monarch must be a Lutheran. The Dutch Royal Family have historically been members of the Dutch Reformed Church, which became the Protestant Church in the Netherlands in 2004. There is no law in the Netherlands stipulating what religion the monarch must espouse although until 1983 the constitution stipulated that marriage to a Catholic meant loss of rights to the throne and there remains a requirement that potential heirs must seek parliamentary approval before marriage in order to retain rights of succession. No other country requires the sovereign to take an oath or make a declaration to maintain and protect the Protestant religion.

Current discussion

There is much discussion about whether the various legal requirements which privilege Protestantism and make the monarch its particular protector have any place today. It is part of a wider debate about whether Christianity as a whole or religion more generally should be favoured in what is a much more secular and pluralistic society than when these laws were framed. Calls to end the Act of Settlement's ban on a Roman Catholic succeeding to the throne, made on the grounds of human rights and eliminating religious prejudice, are often coupled with a demand for dropping the coronation oath, the Scottish oath and the Accession Declaration or at least altering them so that they are not just focused on the maintenance of Protestantism. Even among those who feel that the links between the monarchy and Christianity should still be kept, there is unease about the particular privileging of Protestantism. Adrian Leak, an Anglican priest and writer, has suggested that 'the ancient oath taken by King Edgar in 973 that "the Church of God and the whole Christian people shall have true peace at all times" would suffice.'[8] There is a wider question about whether the coronation oath should continue to favour Christianity over other religions. The report of the Commission on the future of multi-ethnic Britain set up by the Home Secretary and published in 2000 cited it as one of the features of national life that is discriminatory against other faiths.

Under the direction of Robert Hazell and Bob Morris, the Constitution Unit at University College, London, has undertaken detailed study of the Scottish oath, the Accession Declaration oath and the coronation oath and made various suggestions for their redrafting, ranging from minimal changes that would still include reference to the Protestant religion but add mention of freedom for all religious beliefs to a more radical one consistent with the Defender of Faith role discussed in Chapter 11: 'Will you to your power maintain tolerance and freedom, including religious tolerance, and will you seek to uphold the rights of all your peoples to observe their different religions and beliefs without fear of persecution?'.[9] Pointing out that it is ultimately the government that must decide on whether to keep these oaths, and if so, in what form, the Unit further recommends that if there is no political will to legislate for their abolition or to change them, the government should provide a background statement putting them in their historical context. This could be included in a general announcement about coronation arrangements as well as in official and approved souvenir programmes, and accompanied by extensive background briefing for the media. As things stand,

> There is a patent gap between fiction and reality: the sovereign is in no position personally to govern anything or protect any religion – even one that he is required to profess. It could be argued, consequently, that the time has come to relieve sovereigns of obligations they cannot discharge, to separate the secular from the religious where they overlap and require sovereigns simply to observe the constitution of the day, seeking God's help to do so if they personally so wish.[10]

Chapter 10

RELATIONS WITH CHURCHES

The monarch has a close relationship which is set down in law with two specific Christian denominations, the Church of England and the Church of Scotland. The relationship is vastly different in each case, with the sovereign being supreme governor of the Church of England but just an ordinary if much valued member of the Church of Scotland. This strange double allegiance, involving the monarch in switching from Anglicanism to Presbyterianism on crossing the Anglo-Scottish border, is, like so much else, a direct result of the Glorious Revolution of 1688-9 and its aftermath.

In marked contrast to the majority of their subjects, recent British sovereigns have been generally assiduous in their regular attendance at church, not least Queen Elizabeth II who hardly missed a Sunday service throughout her seventy year reign. For much of the year they have worshipped quietly and relatively privately in one of the royal chapels in London or Windsor, particularly in recent decades in the Chapel of All Saints, in the grounds of the Royal Lodge, Windsor Great Park, which was built in 1825 for George IV. Since Victoria's reign, for six weeks or so during the later summer while resident in Balmoral, monarch, consort and other members of the royal family have joined the Sunday morning congregation at Crathie Kirk.

More recently, they have worshipped on Christmas Day at the parish church of St Mary Magdalene in Sandringham, Norfolk. During periods of royal residence in Holyrood Palace, Edinburgh, the nearby Canongate Kirk at the bottom of the Royal Mile is the preferred place of worship.

Membership and maintenance of the Church of England

The 1701 Act of Settlement provides 'that whosoever shall hereafter come to the possession of this Crown shall join in communion with the Church of England as by law established'. This means that the sovereign must be a communicant member of the established Anglican church. As we have already noted (page 173), it is not only in the United Kingdom that the monarch is required to belong to a particular denomination – the crowned heads of Norway, Denmark and Sweden are required to be members of the Lutheran church, although they do not have any role or responsibilities with regard to its governance, maintenance or protection.

Here, by contrast, all sovereigns take an oath at their coronation to 'maintain and preserve inviolably the settlement of the Church of England, and the doctrine worship, discipline, and government thereof, as by law established in England.' Charles I was the first monarch to be required to make such a commitment at his coronation, although in his case it was simply to 'maintain the true profession of the Gospel established by the Church of England'. The oath taken by Charles II at his coronation did not include any specific reference to the Church of England and simply referred to 'the true profession of the Gospel'. It was only after the 1707 Act of Union that the specific requirement to maintain and preserve the Church of England was brought into the coronation oath and it has remained there ever since.

Within a few days of assuming the throne King Charles III made reference both to his membership of the Church of England and his statutory commitment to uphold it. In his first address to the nation, televised on the day after Elizabeth II died, he spoke of his responsibilities towards the Church of England 'in which my own faith is so deeply rooted'. In his address to faith leaders gathered at Buckingham Palace a week later he described himself as 'a committed Anglican' and a member of the Church of England' and went on to say: 'at my coronation I will take an oath relating to the settlement of the Church of England'.

Supreme Governor

The notion of a state church with the country's ruler as its supreme governor essentially derives from the Reformation, even if it was anticipated to some extent in ancient Israel and in the Middle Ages. The principle of royal supremacy over national churches was hammered out by Martin Luther and other sixteenth-century reformers who promoted the ideal of a godly prince ruling a godly nation to counter papal claims of absolute sovereignty over a universal church. It was taken up with particular enthusiasm in England where kings had long been engaged in tussles with the papacy over control of ecclesiastical affairs and appointments.

The monarch's headship of the Church of England was a key part of the Reformation settlement. It was established in three acts passed by Parliament in 1534: the Annates Act which deprived the Pope of his power to appoint bishops, the Act for the Submission of Clergy by which the church in England surrendered its legislative independence to the Crown and the Supremacy Act which declared King Henry VIII 'the only supreme head in earth of the Church of England' with full authority to deal with abuses and intervene in its affairs. These acts effectively gave the English Crown powers similar to those which had been exercised by Holy Roman emperors from the time of Constantine. Royal supremacy over the church was abandoned by the Catholic Queen Mary but reinstated by Elizabeth I, who modified the monarch's title from 'Supreme Head' to 'Supreme Governor', which it has remained ever since.

Among the roles which the sovereign undertakes as Supreme Governor of the Church of England is the appointment of bishops and deans. Elizabeth II's last action in this role shortly before her death was the approval of new bishops of Liverpool, Newcastle and Beverley and a new dean of Canterbury whose names had been passed to her. Previous monarchs took a more hands-on approach to ecclesiastical appointments. Victoria used her influence wherever possible to secure the preferment to the episcopal bench of moderate Broad Churchmen rather than Tractarians or extreme Evangelicals. 'It is by such appointments alone', she told Benjamin Disraeli, 'that we can hope to strengthen the tottering fabric of the established church. The extreme evangelical school do the established church as much harm as the high church.'[1] The Jewish Prime Minister, who was not particularly interested in matters ecclesiastical, found the Queen's hands-on approach to episcopal appointments somewhat frustrating. On one visit to Balmoral he telegraphed his secretary 'Ecclesiastical affairs rage here. Send me Crockford's directory. I must be armed'.[2]

Nowadays nominations for new bishops and deans are made by the Crown Nominations Commission and then passed via Downing Street to Buckingham Palace for final approval by the monarch. There were suggestions some decades ago that the monarch should once again exercise a more direct hands-on role with regard to senior appointments in the Church of England. A committee set up by the Church's General Synod in 1992 found that the sovereign's involvement in the appointment of archbishops, diocesan bishops and deans was greatly valued and it recommended that senior church appointments be made directly by the monarch and not by the prime minister through the mechanism of what was then called the Crown Appointments Committee. The committee felt that such a move would preserve the advantages of establishment and maintain the symbolic role of the sovereign as Supreme Governor, while bypassing the essentially political process and apparatus that many in the Church of England found offensive. Its recommendation was not accepted by General Synod, however, and would, indeed have been constitutionally improper. The sovereign can only act on the advice of a responsible minister and this principle applies to his or her role as supreme governor of the Church of England as much as to other aspects of being head of state.

For their part new bishops kneel before the monarch and swear allegiance following their consecration. The first English Prayer Book of 1549 included a prayer for the sovereign to be said in parish churches every Sunday. It asked God 'so to rule the heart of thy chosen servant, our king/queen and governor, that s/he, knowing whose minister s/he is, may above all things seek thine honour and glory'. Prayers for the monarch and the royal family are included in *Common Worship*, the Church of England's main service book, but they appear in a section entitled 'Prayers for Various Occasions' and in many churches are only used rarely.

Elizabeth II took her role as Supreme Governor extremely seriously and also took a genuine and deep interest in the affairs of the Church of England. In 1970, she inaugurated and addressed its new legislative body, the General Synod, made up of 483 members arranged into three houses: bishops, clergy and laity. For the rest of her reign she continued to undertake this task every five years at the opening sessions of new General Synods following diocesan elections.

Royal peculiars and the Chapel Royal

There remains one area where the monarch still retains slightly more direct control over appointments and other matters in the Church of England. The rather charmingly named royal peculiars, which include Westminster Abbey and the chapels in St James's Palace, Hampton Court, Windsor and the Tower of London, come under the jurisdiction of the Crown and not under the usual diocesan system. A committee set up to look into their management in

2001 recommended the establishment of a standing commission to which the monarch would delegate visitorial functions and which would act as a permanent body to advise the sovereign on their management. Although the committee's report was presented in the newspapers under such headlines as 'Queen may lose control of her five chapels' and 'Queen to loosen grip on Abbey', it specifically commended the principle of continuing independence for the royal peculiars and described them as 'a heritage that should be loved and preserved'. The royal peculiars remain independent and provide a tangible reminder of the sovereign's close relationship with the established church. Elizabeth II did on occasions make her views felt on the nature of worship in Westminster Abbey, particularly in respect of the Commonwealth Day service (see page 197).

The monarch is served by a number of chaplains who form the ecclesiastical branch of the royal household known as the Chapel Royal. Like so much surrounding the Crown, this has ancient origins. Records from the court of Edward the Confessor point to as many as twenty clergy fulfilling the role of royal presbyters. The establishment in 635 by King Sigbert of East Anglia of a school to train boys in singing the divine office has been taken as marking the origins of the body of choristers, known as the Gentlemen and Children of the Chapel Royal, who still sing regularly in the chapel of St James's Palace and at royal and state occasions, the boys standing out in their splendid scarlet coats fringed with gold braid.

The Chapel Royal underwent considerable expansion during the Middle Ages and by Henry V's reign had a strength of 27, of whom at least half were in priests' orders and the rest made up of choristers and clerks. The entire Chapel Royal travelled with the king and the English army to France where they celebrated Mass on the night before the Battle of Agincourt in 1415. The famous Agincourt Song was almost certainly composed by a member of the Chapel Royal, possibly in thanksgiving for the victory at the battle and to be sung at Henry's triumphant homecoming. The Chapel Royal remains an important part of the royal household, presided over by the Dean, an office usually held by the Bishop of London, and a full-time Sub-Dean.

Current debate and discussion with regard to Supreme Governorship

The desirability of the monarch remaining Supreme Governor of the Church of England has been much discussed and debated over recent decades. Several voices both from within and outside the Church of England have argued that it is now an anachronism but others have eloquently defended it. It is bound up with the wider question of whether the Church of England should remain established.

Debate over the issue of the Supreme Governorship was clouded during the early 1990s by irrelevant speculation as to whether the then Prince of Wales, as a divorced person, or in the event of re-marrying after divorce, as in the event he did, could properly assume that role on becoming king. The matter was admirably put into perspective by John Habgood, the then Archbishop of York.

> Sovereigns are not required to be saints …
> Nevertheless, is the Supreme Governor of
> the Church of England required to be at least
> as morally sober as an archbishop? If supreme

governorship were the same as spiritual leadership the answer might be yes. But this would represent a serious misunderstanding. A monarch's personal involvement in the Church is welcome. The role of Supreme Governor, however, is not personal but institutional.

The monarch is the visible representative of the unity and identity of the nation, and it is the Church's commitment to the nation, and responsibility for its spiritual welfare, which is symbolised by supreme governorship. It would be theoretically possible to hold to the symbol even if in personal terms the monarch only fulfilled the minimum requirement of belonging to the Protestant succession.

As Habgood made clear, the monarch's role as Supreme Governor is constitutional and is not in any way dependent on the personal faith or behaviour of the sovereign. There have been suggestions that the title should be changed to reflect a less authoritarian and more participatory relationship between sovereign and church. The late David Edwards, a senior churchman and church historian, reviewing an earlier book of mine on the spiritual dimension of monarchy published in 2002, wrote: 'It seems right that the monarch should be a protector of the Church to which the majority of the English still turn when wanting a church (I mean the Church of England) – but isn't the role better described as being the Church's 'Senior Member'?[4]

Such a title would make the monarch's relationship with the Church of England more similar to that with the Church of Scotland. The title 'Supreme Governor' may seem somewhat overbearing and archaic, although, as several ecclesiastical and constitutional experts have pointed out, it is an aspect of the wider constitutional role of the Head of State and reflects the source and seat of sovereignty in our country in matters spiritual as well as temporal. The Anglican priest and theologian, Paul Avis, has pointed to the benefits that the Supreme Governorship offers in terms of having a lay person in a position of responsibility and leadership in the national church.[5] Whatever the title, there is much to be said for a symbolic acknowledgement of the Church of England's role as a broad, capacious national church and, indeed, for a continuation of the practice of archbishops and diocesan bishops signifying their loyalty and allegiance to the Crown on appointment as an expression of their commitment to minister to the whole nation and not just the faithful few who are church members and attenders.

The Monarch's relationship with and responsibility towards the Church of Scotland

The Church of England is not the only denomination with which the monarch has a special and close relationship. Almost the first official utterance made by the sovereign after his or her accession is the so-called 'Scottish oath' undertaking 'to inviolably maintain and preserve the Government, Worship, Discipline, Rights and Privileges of the Church of Scotland' under the terms of the 1707 Act passed by the Scottish Parliament, and ratified in the Treaty and Act of Union, for securing the Protestant Religion and Presbyterian Church Government'. Charles III took this oath at the meeting of the Accession Council on 10 September 2022 and specifically alluded to it when he spoke to leaders of different faiths six days later. As has already been pointed out, the close relationship between the Crown and the Presbyterian Church of Scotland is a direct consequence of the Glorious Revolution, the failure of the Scottish bishops to support the new Protestant succession and the threat of Jacobite insurrection bringing Catholic Stuarts to the throne again.

The sovereign has never held the title of supreme head or governor of the post-Reformation reformed Church of Scotland. Holding that such titles belonged to Jesus Christ alone, its General Assembly in 1568 ordered the pulping of all copies of a book on the downfall of the Roman Church because it referred to the recently crowned James VI as 'supreme head of the primitive kirk'. When a Scottish Oath of Supremacy was drawn up in 1572, it avoided the English formula that the monarch was supreme governor 'in all spiritual or ecclesiastical things or causes as in all things temporal' and spoke rather of him as 'the only supreme governor of this realm, as well in things temporal as in the conservation and purgation of religion'.[6]

The clearest statement of the Church of Scotland's doctrine on its relationship with the monarch was delivered by Alexander Melville, the true architect of Scottish Presbyterianism. In a celebrated encounter with James VI at Falkland Palace in 1596, he took hold of the king's gown, called him 'God silly vassal' and lectured him on what became known as the 'two kingdoms theory':

I must tell you, there are two kings and two kingdoms in Scotland: there is King James the head of this Commonwealth, and there is Christ Jesus the King of the Church, whose subject

James the Sixth is, and of whose kingdom he is not a king, nor a lord, nor a head, but a member.

We will yield to you your place, and give you all due obedience; but again I say, you are not the head of the church: you cannot give us that eternal life which we seek for even in this world, and you cannot deprive us of it. When you were in your swaddling clothes, Christ Jesus reigned freely in this land in spite of all his enemies.[7]

Although the Church of Scotland would not call the monarch its Supreme Governor, he or she was given the right to decide the time and the place for its general assemblies and to attend them. To this day, the Church of Scotland's annual general assembly in Edinburgh is attended and opened either by the sovereign or by his or her representative, the Lord High Commissioner, appointed by the monarch 'to supply our presence and to hold our place'.

Crathie Church and its place in royal affections

The close and affectionate relationship between the monarchy and Scotland's national church has perhaps most clearly been expressed over the last 150 years or more in the sovereign's regular participation in worship in the local parish church when resident throughout the late summer at Balmoral. Two queens, Victoria and Elizabeth, found the style of worship at Crathie Kirk particularly congenial.

The distinctly Protestant and Low Church hue of Victoria's Christianity, influenced both by her mother's evangelicalism and her husband's Lutheranism, has already been noted. She found the worship in the Presbyterian Church of Scotland much more to her taste than that in the Anglican Church of England, developing a particular affection for the Sunday morning services at Crathie Parish Church which she rebuilt in 1893, the first church building in the United Kingdom personally paid for by a monarch since the Reformation. Victoria's regular attendance there met with strong Anglican disapproval, as expressed in the *English Churchman*: 'Her Majesty may, when she crosses the Tweed, doff Spitalfields silks and don Scotch tartan, but she may not put off her Churchmanship and adopt Scottish Presbyterianism without forfeiting her character as a member of the Catholic Church.'[8]

Leading Anglicans were horrified that when in Scotland the Queen not only attended a Presbyterian church but also shared in the sacrament there. When she first received communion at Crathie Kirk in 1873, it was against the advice of senior English clerics. 'The Queen', her private secretary, Sir Henry Ponsonby, noted with some irritation,

> needless to say carried out her own decision, in spite of warnings and even objections from the Archbishop of Canterbury, the Dean of Westminster and the Dean of Windsor. No report was allowed in the Court Circular but the ecclesiastical and legal side of the question produced a mass of correspondence with which her Private Secretary was very much bored.[9]

Scottish ministers not surprisingly took a rather different view. Preaching in St Giles' Cathedral the Sunday after her death, Dr Cameron Lees said 'To see her at Crathie side by side with the poorest in the glen, taking with them the symbols of our common redemption, was a sight which those who witnessed can never forget'.[10] A Deeside farmer put it even more eloquently. On being assured by his minister that she had indeed received Communion sitting unobtrusively with her tenants and servants around the Lord's table, he exclaimed 'That would make a man die for her!'[11]

Victoria's partiality for the Church of Scotland extended to its preachers. Requiring that sermons preached before her be 'orthodox, short and interesting', she generally demanded that no preacher exceed twenty minutes. However, this was waived in the case of several Scottish ministers, notably her own favourite chaplain, Norman Macleod, who once preached before her for 47 minutes only to be told that she wished he had gone on for longer. Other Scottish preachers who shared Macleod's combination of liberal broad churchmanship and vigorous muscular Christianity were similarly indulged. When Cosmo Gordon Lang, the future Archbishop of Canterbury, who as vicar of Portsea regularly preached at Osborne House and was himself the son of a Church of Scotland minister, complained of this favouritism, the Queen replied, 'When English dignitaries can preach as well as Scottish ministers, I will let them go on as long as they like'.[12]

It was ten days after first receiving Communion at Crathie that Victoria started her campaign to curb ritualistic practices in the Church of England (pages 171-2). Twenty years later, in another use of the royal prerogative, she intervened to protect her beloved Church of Scotland, refusing to sanction the Queen's Speech to Parliament in 1894 if it included a commitment to its disestablishment which had been in the manifesto of the recently elected Liberal Government. The religious affairs correspondent of the

Scotsman commented, 'personally, I have no doubt that the Queen saved the historic Church of Scotland'.[13]

Like her great-great grandmother, Queen Elizabeth II had a fondness for the simplicity and dignity of Presbyterian worship in the Church of Scotland There were few places where her deep Christian faith was more evident than in Crathie Church where she attended worship every Sunday together with the local congregation while resident in Balmoral. In 2002 I had the privilege of being invited to preach there and to stay over the weekend as a guest at Balmoral, a practice instituted by Victoria so that she could spend even more time with her favourite Church of Scotland ministers. Along with sitting up half the night discussing the subject of Christianity and the environment with the Duke of Edinburgh, one of my most vivid recollections of the weekend is of looking across from my seat by the pulpit at the royal pew during the service and seeing Elizabeth II enthusiastically singing a Scots metrical psalm which she clearly knew by heart. It was indeed fitting as well as poignant that she should have died just across the River Dee from her beloved Crathie Kirk.

Relations with other churches

Although understandably it has been with the Church of England and Church of Scotland that British monarchs have had the closest relations and in their churches that they have mostly worshipped, several sovereigns have also reached out to other denominations with both Victoria and Elizabeth being particularly keen to heal the long-standing post-Reformation animosity between the Crown and the Roman Catholic church.

Although she abhorred Anglo-Catholic ritualism in the Church of England, Victoria has no animus against Roman Catholics. Indeed, a contemporary pointed out that 'she liked Roman Catholics very much better than Anglican Ritualists.'[14] She deplored the no-Popery riots which followed the restoration of the English hierarchy, declaring 'I cannot bear to hear the violent abuse of the Catholic religion, which is so painful and cruel to the many good and innocent Roman Catholics.'[15] Towards the end of her reign she sent the Duke of Norfolk as her envoy to the Vatican to assure the Pope of her 'sincere friendship and unfeigned respect and esteem'. This personal gesture, apparently made at her own initiative, did much to thaw the traditionally frosty relations between the British Crown and Rome.

The unease felt by both Edward VII and George V about the strongly anti-Catholic tone of the accession declaration required by the 1688 Bill of Rights has already been noted (page 172). Edward VII had a strong personal interest in Catholicism. On a visit to Rome in 1903 he met Pope Leo XIII in a private capacity, the Cabinet having advised against an official visit. Towards the end of his life he visited Lourdes. One of his last visitors as he lay dying was Father Cyril Foster, Catholic chaplain to the Irish Guards, and there have been suggestions that he received the king into the Catholic church on his deathbed.[16]

Elizabeth II's reign saw a much greater level of engagement between the British Crown and the Roman Catholic church than any previous one since the Reformation, much of it apparently prompted by the Queen's personal initiative. In 1995 she became the first monarch in 400 years to attend a Catholic liturgy when she went to a service of vespers in Westminster

Cathedral to mark its centenary. She subsequently made a generous personal donation to the giant millennium cross erected in the piazza outside the mother church of English Catholicism. The last foray made by the much loved English Catholic leader Cardinal Basil Hume from his sick bed during his final illness in 1999 was to visit Buckingham Palace and receive from the Queen the Order of Merit to which she had personally appointed him. She also invited his successor as Cardinal Archbishop of Westminster and leader of English Catholics, Cormac Murphy-O'Connor, to preach before her at Sandringham. It was widely reported that she had very much hoped to pray with Pope John Paul II during her visit to the Vatican in October 2000 but that this had been vetoed by senior figures in the Church of England. In September 2010 she warmly welcomed Pope Benedict XVI to the palace of Holyrood in Edinburgh at the start of his state visit to the United Kingdom, telling him, 'your presence here today reminds us of our common Christian heritage' and paying tribute to the Catholic Church's 'special contribution' to helping the poorest and most vulnerable around the world. Another symbolic gesture of reconciliation towards Rome came in 2016 when she approved a wreath to be placed on the tomb of the Old Pretender in St Peter's Basilica on the 250th anniversary of his death.

As Prince of Wales, King Charles sought a close relationship with the Roman Catholic church. When he and Diana, Princess of Wales, met Pope John Paul II in Rome in 1985, he expressed a strong desire to attend Mass in St Peter's celebrated by the pope. Arrangements were made for him and the princess to attend a private mass in the pope's chapel, although not to receive communion, but this was called off after the Queen expressed unease in a conversation with her son. In Catherine Pepinster's words, 'the Queen herself remained resolute that relations with Rome could only go so far, although her meetings with Popes were warm, as has been their admiration for her'.[17] Charles did, however, receive a rosary from John Paul which he is said to have kept by his bedside. His strong interest in the liturgy and teaching of the Orthodox Church was reflected in his decision to begin the Millennium Year of 2000 with a retreat in the monastery on Mount Athos in Greece.

Commonwealth services and visits and jubilee celebrations have brought the monarchy into contact with black Pentecostal churches and their gospel choirs. Perhaps the denominations with which the monarchy have had least contact are the historic Free churches. Following an article I wrote in *The Times* immediately after her death about Elizabeth II's eirenic faith and ecumenical instincts, I received an email from a minister in the Congregational Federation questioning whether she had ever attended worship in a nonconformist church in England or a Welsh chapel. He went on: 'Indeed one wonders whether any British monarch has ever attended worship in a nonconformist church – Methodist, Baptist, URC etc.'[18] I think he may have a point. All I could say in reply was that when I was bidding farewell to her after my stay in Balmoral, the Queen told me that the following week a Methodist would be preaching at Crathie – 'so that should be fun', she said.

Chapter 11

DEFENDER OF
(THE) FAITH

The monarch's role as Defender of the Faith has been through one major change of meaning and is currently undergoing another. Originally bestowed on Henry VIII by the Pope for the king's robust defence of the Catholic faith, since the Reformation it has generally been associated with the sovereign's role as protector of Protestantism. Over recent decades, partly as a result of statements by Charles III when Prince of Wales and initiatives by Elizabeth II, it has been given an increasingly broad interpretation in royal circles and come to have an interfaith dimension. A Home Office commissioned report in 2000 on religious discrimination paid tribute to the Royal Family's 'public association with the positive development of the UK as a multi-faith society'.[1]

Origins of the title

The title *Fidei Defensor*, which appears abbreviated as FID. DEF. on the £2 coin and simply as F.D. on other coins of the realm, was granted to Henry VIII by Pope Leo X in 1521 in recognition of the king's defence of the seven traditional sacraments of the Catholic Church in a theological pamphlet attacking the teachings of Martin Luther and other Reformers which appeared under the king's name but had effectively been ghost-written by his Chancellor, Thomas More. Fourteen years later More went to the scaffold for refusing to recognise Henry VIII as head of the English church. Pope Paul II revoked the title after Henry's break with Rome but the English parliament conferred it on Henry together with the title of Supreme Head of the Church of England and it has continued to be used by and about all English and British monarchs since. Although its meaning has never been precisely defined, it is generally taken to relate to the sovereign's role in defending the Protestant faith, a somewhat ironic interpretation given its origins.

Queen Elizabeth II's outreach to non-Christian faiths

When Elizabeth II came to the throne in 1952 the United Kingdom was a relatively homogeneous, largely white and predominantly Christian country with a very small proportion of the population adhering to other faiths. The transition to a multi-faith and multi-cultural society was one of the major changes to take place during her reign. It was embraced and indeed welcomed by the Queen, thanks in large part to the broad, open nature of her own deep Christian faith with its particular attachment to the values of tolerance and reconciliation, and also to her strong attachment to the Commonwealth, itself a pioneer inter-faith community.

A relatively early example of royal leadership in this area came in the mid-1960s when the leaders of the Commonwealth Day service asked for it to be made a multi-faith celebration, reflecting the many different faiths represented in the countries of the Commonwealth. Eric Abbott, Dean of Westminster Abbey which had hosted the service since 1963, was uneasy about this and the service was moved to the secular venue of the Guildhall in the City of London. As a royal peculiar, the Abbey comes under the jurisdiction of the Crown and the Queen used her direct influence to make clear to the Dean that she wished the service to be restored to the Abbey and to have an interfaith dimension. He somewhat reluctantly agreed, on condition that it was called an observance rather than a service. In the words of Catherine Pepinster, 'It was a moment when the Queen led and the Anglican primacy later followed'.[2] In 1997 Elizabeth requested that interfaith representatives be present at the service held in the Abbey to mark her golden wedding anniversary. Invitations were sent to the Chief Rabbi and the Director of the Muslim College.

The Queen's interest in other faiths and her commitment to respect and dialogue between faith communities was particularly apparent in her Christmas broadcasts. In the 2000 broadcast where she notably made a very direct and personal statement about her own Christian faith, she went on to say, 'Of course religion can be divisive, but the Bible, the Koran and the sacred texts of the Jews and Hindus, Buddhists and Sikhs, are all sources of divine inspiration and practical guidance passed down through the generations'. Her 2001 Christmas broadcast in the aftermath of the 9/11 attack on the World Trade Center in New York reflected on the values of communities and a sense of belonging:

A sense of belonging to a group, which has in common the same desire for a fair and ordered society, helps to overcome differences and misunderstanding by reducing prejudice, ignorance and fear.

We all have something to learn from one another, whatever our faith - be it Christian or Jewish, Muslim, Buddhist, Hindu or Sikh - whatever our background, whether we be young or old, from town or countryside.

In his book *Chosen People* Clifford Longley contrasted this broadcast with Rudi Giuliani's farewell speech as mayor of New York just two days earlier. While Giuliani explicitly invoked patriotism, saying that the test of Americanism is how much you believe in America 'because we are like a religion really. A secular religion. We believe in ideas and ideals', the Queen never mentioned Britain or Britishness but rather spoke in broad terms of the importance of faith and of communities and, in the Christian context, of the church's role 'to give meaning to moments of intense human experience through prayer, symbol and ceremony'. Her quiet calm plea for tolerance and respect contrasted with Giuliani's strident beating of the patriotic drum.[3]

In 2002, the year of her golden jubilee, Elizabeth II became the first British monarch to visit a mosque when she accepted an invitation from Scunthorpe's Islamic Centre. Afzal Khan, who presented her with a copy of the Quran, told the BBC's Religion editor, Aleem Maqbool, 'It was in the months after the 9/11 attacks and we were suffering. We were frightened and needed support from someone to tell us we are part of British society too. That support came from the Queen. After her visit, we felt like it didn't matter if anybody called us terrorists. We were still

British.'[4] As part of her jubilee celebrations that year she also visited a Hindu Temple in London, a Sikh Gurdwara in Leicester and the Manchester Jewish Museum. In 2015 she visited the Nazi concentration camp at Bergen-Belsen in Germany accompanied by Ephraim Mirvis, Chief Rabbi of the United Hebrew Congregations of Great Britain and the Commonwealth, who commented that 'The memory of the Holocaust remains such a fundamental aspect of modern Jewish identity that the Queen's journey to memorialise the victims will be viewed as tremendously significant by Jewish communities across the world.' It was one of several meetings that he had with the Queen which made clear to him that her interest in his faith went far beyond duty: 'I could see the extent of her connection with Jews and Judaism and her concern for the safety of Jews'.[5]

Elizabeth II's address to both Houses of Parliament on the occasion of her Golden Jubilee in April 2002, said to have been more personal and revealing of her own feelings than many of her speeches, noted that 'the consolidation of our richly multicultural and multi-faith society, a major development since 1952, is being achieved remarkably peacefully and with much goodwill.' In her address she characterized the British as ' a moderate, pragmatic people, outward-looking and open-minded', a phrase that well described her own position on many issues, and identified fairness and tolerance as the two enduring traditions in which the country should take most pride. Her 2004 Christmas broadcast reiterated this theme, affirming that 'tolerance and fair play remain strong British values'. It was noticeable that the service of thanksgiving to mark her 80th birthday in St Paul's Cathedral in June 2006 included a procession of world faith representatives and prayers delivered by the High Commissioners from Pakistan, Nigeria, New Guinea and Barbados, reflecting her passionate commitment to the Commonwealth and its rich mixture of faiths, races and cultures.

Perhaps the most significant statement that the Queen made in this area came in a reception held at Lambeth Palace, hosted by the Archbishop of Canterbury, to mark the start of her Diamond Jubilee in 2012. Before an audience of senior church leaders and representatives of the Bahai, Buddhist, Hindu, Jain, Jewish, Muslim, Sikh and Zoroastrian faiths, she reflected on the 'significant position of the Church of England in our nation's life' and went on to say:

> The concept of our established Church is occasionally misunderstood and, I believe, commonly under-appreciated. Its role is not to defend Anglicanism to the exclusion of other religions. Instead, the Church has a duty to protect the free practice of all faiths in this country.
>
> It certainly provides an identity and spiritual dimension for its own many adherents. But also, gently and assuredly, the Church of England has created an environment for other faith communities and indeed people of no faith to live freely. Woven into the fabric of this country, the Church has helped to build a better society – more and more in active co-operation for the common good with those of other faiths.[6]

Here was the Church's Supreme Governor calling for it to assume the role of defender and protector of all faiths, providing an umbrella under which non-Christians could safely shelter. She was also, by implication, claiming this role for the monarch, as Supreme Governor and Defender of the Faith. It was a role that she continued to put into practice to the very end of her reign. In 2019 she hosted a reception at Buckingham Palace to celebrate the work of different faith groups throughout the UK in bringing local communities together. In April 2020, in the middle of the Covid pandemic, she recorded her first ever Easter broadcast. While its specific focus was on the Christian Easter message of hope based on Christ's resurrection, the overall theme was much wider:

> Many religions have festivals which celebrate light overcoming darkness. Such occasions are often accompanied by the lighting of candles. They seem to speak to every culture, and appeal to people of all faiths, and of none. They are lit on birthday cakes and to mark family anniversaries, when we gather happily around a source of light. It unites us.

Several influences underlay Elizabeth II's clear and practical interfaith commitment. Alongside her attachment to the Commonwealth and its modelling of a multi-faith and multicultural community was the strong support and encouragement she received in her ventures into this area from her husband. Prince Philip had a longstanding interest in interfaith matters, which he put into practice in the development of St George's House, Windsor in the early 1960s and the creation of the Alliance of Religions and Conservation in 1995. Speaking on BBC radio shortly after Prince Philip's death in 2021, Jonathan Romain, a prominent Reform rabbi and leader of the Maidenhead Synagogue in Berkshire who was much involved in discussions in St George's House in its early days, said: 'We talk now of interfaith as a commonplace but 40 years ago it wasn't. Prince Philip was someone who first endorsed it. He also gave out a clear message that people who worship in a synagogue, mosque or gurdwara are as much a part of British society as those who worship in church.'[7]

Elizabeth was also undoubtedly influenced by her son Charles, whose well-publicised views about the monarch's role as Defender of (the) Faith are discussed below. But what principally led her to engage with and embrace other faiths was the nature of her own Christian faith. She perhaps spelled it out most clearly in her 2014 Christmas broadcast:

> For me, the life of Jesus Christ, the Prince of Peace, whose birth we celebrate today, is an inspiration and an anchor in my life. A role model of reconciliation and forgiveness, he stretched out his hands in love, acceptance and healing. Christ's example has taught me to seek to respect and value all people of whatever faith or none.

The values that the Queen singled out as central to Christ's life and ministry – reconciliation, forgiveness, love, acceptance, healing and respect for all people of whatever faith or none – were the ones which she sought to live by and to champion throughout her reign. Hers was a deep but also a very open Christian faith in which tolerance and respect for others, and admiration for the teachings and practices of other faiths, were central. The Chief Rabbi's prayer on her passing described her as 'a defender of faith' – so she was just as much as she was a staunch Defender of the (Christian) Faith.

Defender of Faith

In conversation with Jonathan Dimbleby in a 1994 television documentary *Charles: The Private Man, the Public Role* the then Prince Charles discussed his long-standing belief 'that the Catholic subjects of the sovereign are equally as important as the Anglican ones, as the Protestant ones. I think that the Islamic subjects or the Hindu subjects or the Zoroastrian subjects of the sovereign are of equal and vital importance.' [8] He went on to provide his own novel interpretation of the monarch's traditional role as Defender of the Faith:

> I personally would rather see it as Defender of Faith, not the Faith, because it (Defender of the Faith) means just one particular interpretation of the Faith, which I think is sometimes something that causes a deal of a problem. It has done for hundreds of years. People have fought each other to the death over these things, which seems to me a peculiar waste of people's energy, when we're all actually aiming for the same ultimate goal, I think. So I would much rather it was seen as defending faith itself which is so often under threat in our day where, you know, the whole concept of faith itself or anything beyond this existence, beyond life itself is considered almost old-fashioned and irrelevant. [9]

Further clarifying his position, the Prince went on to say that for him Defender of Faith meant being 'Defender of the Divine in existence, the pattern of the Divine which is, I think, in all of us but which, because we are human beings, can be expressed in so many different ways'.[10]

These statements by the heir to the throne about one of the monarch's best-known titles, its continuing spiritual significance, and how it might best be interpreted today, caused a considerable sensation in the media. Missing their main point, commentators almost without exception chose to take the Prince's remarks as suggesting that he wanted to sever the links between the monarchy and Church of England. The *Sunday Times*, which published an exclusive preview of the prince's remarks before the Dimbleby documentary was shown, set the tone of press coverage by running under the headline 'Charles plans to break royal link with church' a front-page story which began:

> The Prince of Wales is planning to end the 450-year-old role of the monarch as head of the Church of England and Defender of the Faith. Charles believes that when he becomes king he should be a figurehead for all religions in Britain, including Roman Catholics and Muslims, and that the church should be disestablished.[11]

In fact there was nothing whatsoever about disestablishment, nor indeed about the royal relationship with the Church of England, in the Prince of Wales' remarks. As already noted, it is governed by the Coronation Oath and the sovereign's role as the Church's Supreme Governor.

DEFENDER OF (THE) FAITH

Jonathan Dimbleby was quite wrong to say in his book based on the television programme that Prince Charles' remarks about becoming Defender of Faith 'expressed strong sentiments about the relationship of the sovereign to the Church of England'.[12] They did nothing of the sort. The prince made no allusion to the monarch's role of Supreme Governor. He was not addressing the monarchy's constitutional relationship with the established Church of England but rather its role in an increasingly secular and pluralistic society in promoting religious faith in the broadest sense. In 2015, he felt the need to clarify his position in an interview with BBC Radio 2. Pointing out that his views had been misinterpreted, he said: 'As I tried to describe, I mind about the inclusion of other people's faiths and their freedom to worship in this country. And it's always seemed to me that, while at the same time being Defender of the Faith, you can also be protector of faiths.' He cited the speech made by the Queen at Lambeth Palace in 2012 when, in his words, she had said her role was 'not to defend Anglicanism to the exclusion of other religions. Instead, the Church [of England] has a duty to protect the free practice of all faiths in this country'. He went on, 'I think in that sense she was confirming what I was really trying to say – perhaps not very well – all those years ago.'[13]

Charles' proposed title of 'Defender of Faith' for the monarch was, indeed, essentially expressing and defining the role that his mother had increasingly fulfilled throughout her reign. Like her, he was embracing the multi-faith nature of modern Britain and also seeking to protect freedom of belief and conscience and affirm the fundamental importance of respect and tolerance. Like his mother, he was also inspired by his own Christian beliefs and his genuine interest in the teachings of other faiths and their contribution to the spiritual dimension of life. In his own case, this was particularly true of Islam in which he had a deep and abiding interest. This is much appreciated by British Muslims who have often felt stigmatised over recent decades. In the words of Zara Mohammed, head of the Muslim Council of Britain, the largest group representing the UK's three million Muslims: 'He has given us a lot of confidence. We regard him as an admirer of Islam and a friend of British Muslims. It's brilliant to see how he grasps how the U.K. has changed. He sees a more holistic picture and the power of all faiths and diverse communities working together.'[14]

Charles clearly signalled his determination to pursue the role of 'Defender of Faith' in one of his first speeches as king, made to a reception for 30 faith leaders at Buckingham Palace less than a week after his accession. While clearly identifying his own faith position – 'I am a committed Anglican Christian' – and indicating his support for the Church of England and Church of Scotland as expressed in the accession and coronation oaths, he went on to outline what he sees as an important additional duty on the part of the monarch, 'less formally recognized but to be no less diligently discharged':

It is the duty to protect the diversity of our country, including by protecting the space for Faith itself and its practice through the religions, cultures, traditions and beliefs to which our hearts and minds direct us as individuals. This diversity is not just enshrined in the laws of our country, it is enjoined by my own faith. As a member of the Church of England, my Christian beliefs have love at their very heart. By my most profound convictions, therefore – as well as by my position as Sovereign – I hold myself bound to respect those who follow other spiritual paths, as well as those who seek to live their lives in accordance with secular ideals.

The beliefs that flourish in, and contribute to, our richly diverse society differ. They, and our society, can only thrive through a clear collective commitment to those vital principles of freedom of conscience, generosity of spirit and care for others which are, to me, the essence of our nationhood. I am determined, as King, to preserve and promote those principles across all communities, and for all beliefs, with all my heart.[15]

King Charles' desire to act as 'Defender of Faith' springs in large part from his own overwhelming mission, about which he feels an almost evangelistic zeal, to promote religious belief and a sense of the spiritual and sacred against the prevailing tide of secular materialism and scientific reductionism (see pages 225-8). It also springs from the strong commitment he shares with his mother to religious tolerance and pluralism, and a particular desire to foster understanding between Islam and the West. His understanding of this role is clearly outlined in a remark that he made about King Hussein of Jordan:

King Hussein had the kind of enlightened spirit that was in harmony with those who, in earlier periods of history, were able instinctively to respect the followers of other faiths for their piety and moral character, even if they did not accept them theologically.[16]

This role for the monarch as fount of tolerance and respect for a wide range of beliefs, not from a position of latitudinarian indifference or secular laissez-faire but out of a real sense of the importance of religious faith, has also been articulated by another European sovereign. In a 2016 interview with the German magazine, *Der Spiegel*, Queen Margrethe of Denmark said, 'Under the constitution, as the Danish Queen I am bound to the Lutheran faith, but that does not exclude people of other faiths. On the contrary, I believe that the fact that I am religious brings me closer to anyone with a different faith'.[17]

Publication of data from the 2021 census revealing that less than half the population of England and Wales now identifies as Christian (the figure is 46.2%, down from 59.3% in 2011) has provided further grounds for considering a change in the monarch's role from 'Defender of the Faith' to 'Defender of Faith'. In the words of Rabbi Jonathan Romain, 'Britain is now thoroughly multifaith, and a slight change in the king's title would be a way of acknowledging this transition without diminishing our Christian heritage or disestablishing'.[18]

Chapter 12

SACRED RITUALS AND ENGAGEMENTS IN THE ROYAL CALENDAR

Modern monarchy involves a relentless series of public and private engagements which slot into a full diary and allow little time for rest and reflection. They include overseas tours, visits to open hospitals, schools and factories, inspections of the armed forces, audiences with politicians and foreign heads of state, plus the daily task of getting through the red boxes sent by the Government to 'Reader No.1'. There are also a good number which have a sacred character. This chapter lists and describes the main religious ceremonies and rituals which involve the monarch in the course of the year.

January: Feast of the Epiphany – Offering of the King's Gifts

On the feast of the Epiphany (6 January) there is a service of sung Eucharist in the Chapel Royal in St James's Palace at which offerings of gold, frankincense and myrrh are carried to the altar. This service goes back at least 500 years and is directly modelled on the presentation of gifts to the infant Jesus by the *magi* as recorded in Matthew's Gospel. Until the reign of George III, the sovereign always made these offerings in person but they are now usually carried to the altar on silver gilt salvers by two Gentlemen Ushers led by the Serjeant of the Vestry and escorted by three Yeomen of the Guard. Until 1859 the gold was offered in the form of a small roll of gold leaf. This was changed, at the suggestion of Prince Albert, into a dish of 25 new sovereigns. The frankincense and myrrh, which are provided by the Royal Apothecary, are obtained directly from the Holy Land. After the service, the incense is sent to a local church and the myrrh is sent to the Anglican Benedictine community at Nashdom Abbey to be mixed with the incense prepared there.

March: Commonwealth Day service

On the second Sunday in March representatives of the 54 countries in the Commonwealth attend a service in Westminster Abbey to celebrate the Commonwealth and the monarch's commitment to it. Originally known as Empire Day and established in 1902 to honour Queen Victoria, its name was changed to Commonwealth Day in 1958 and in 1977 it was moved from 24 May, Queen Victoria's birthday. Usually attended by the monarch, it constitutes the largest inter-faith gathering in the United Kingdom with substantial participation from representatives of non-Christian faiths while maintaining the framework of a Christian service of worship. The musical accompaniment, which has come in recent years from black Gospel choirs, steel bands and sitars, is noticeably different from that at most royal and state services.

March or April: Royal Maundy Service

The annual service held on Maundy Thursday in Holy Week at which the sovereign distributes alms to the poor is a powerful symbol of Christian monarchy and specifically of servant kingship modelled on the example of Christ. Its ultimate origins may conceivably lie in the actions of the sixth-century Northumbrian King Oswald in giving pieces of his silver dish to the poor on Easter Day but as a distinct ceremony it seems to have begun around the same time as touching for the king's evil. King John is the first English monarch recorded as having distributed alms to his people in the context of a service on Maundy Thursday, in his case at Knaresborough in Yorkshire in 1210. Three years later at a ceremony in Rochester he gave thirteen pence to thirteen men, a number presumably chosen to represent Jesus and his disciples. The practice was continued by successive monarchs, with Henry IV ordering that the number of recipients of Maundy money, clothes and shoes should correspond with the monarch's age.

During the Royal Maundy service medieval and early Tudor monarchs personally washed the feet of the poor in direct imitation of Jesus' actions with his disciples at the last supper. Mary I is recorded as washing the feet of 41 women as she knelt before them in 1556. As well as giving them 41 pence each, she made additional gifts of bread, fish and clothes, including one of her own gowns. Elizabeth I delegated the task of foot washing to the yeomen of the royal laundry but the Stuart kings revived it and the last monarch personally to wash the feet of the poor was James II. Thereafter the task of washing the Maundy recipients' feet was undertaken by the almoner, an official drawn from the ranks of the royal chaplains whose role originally included gathering food from the royal table and visiting the sick, orphans, widows and prisoners. This part of the Maundy service was dropped in 1754. The monarch's personal participation in the distribution of alms, by now restricted to specially minted silver coins and taking place at the Chapel Royal in London, also lapsed in the nineteenth century. It was reinstated by George V in 1932, although neither he nor George VI participated themselves every year, leaving it to the Lord High Almoner.

Elizabeth II returned to the practice of direct monarchical involvement in the Royal Maundy Service every year and also made the significant innovation of holding it in different cathedrals around the country. The recipients of Maundy money are pensioners of modest income most of whom are selected on the basis of their service to church and community. Each receives a white leather bag containing special Maundy coins and a red leather bag containing ordinary money. There are two readings in the service: John 13:34, 'A new commandment I give unto you, That ye love one another; as I have loved you, that ye also love one another', and Matthew 25.34-40, the parable of the sheep and the goats. They reinforce the Christian inspiration of this service and the ideal of servant monarchy. This is also symbolized by the fact both the Lord High Almoner (currently the Bishop of Worcester) and the sub-almoner, traditionally the sub-dean of the Chapel Royal, wear linen aprons as a reminder of the foot washing ritual inspired by Jesus' own example. Perhaps it can become part of the service again.

SACRED RITUALS AND ENGAGEMENTS

June: Garter Service

The Most Noble Order of the Garter was founded in 1348 by King Edward III inspired by tales of King Arthur and the Knights of the Round Table. It is the oldest and most senior order of chivalry in Britain. As sovereign of the Order, the monarch personally chooses its 24 Companions, male and female, in recognition of their public service. The patron saint of the Order is St George and its spiritual home is St George's Chapel, Windsor, in which every knight is required to display a banner of arms, together with a helmet, crest and sword and an enamelled stall plate.

On Garter Day new Companions are invested by the King with the Order's insignia in the throne room of Windsor Castle. After lunch, all Companions, who include senior members of the Royal Family as well as the sovereign and consort, process on foot wearing dark blue velvet robes and plumed hats from the castle quadrangle to St George's Chapel, accompanied by the Military Knights of Windsor, the Officers of Arms, a detachment from the Yeomen of the Guard and a marching band. There follows a short service conducted by the Register of the Order, the Dean of Windsor, in which new Companions are installed.

June or July every two years: Thistle service

The Scottish equivalent of the Order of the Garter is the Most Ancient and Most Noble Order of The Thistle. Various kings of Scots have been credited with its foundation, including

Achaius in the late eight or early ninth century, Robert the Bruce in the aftermath of the Battle of Bannockburn in 1314, James III in the late fifteenth century and James V in the early sixteenth century. In 1687 James VII issued letters patent 'revising and restoring the Order of the Thistle to its full glory, lustre and magnificence'. His intention was to reward Scottish Catholics for their loyalty. Following his deposition from the throne, the exiled House of Stuart continued to make appointments to the Order which were not recognised by the British crown. Queen Anne began appointing knights again in 1704 and since then the monarch, as sovereign of the Order, has continued this practice, with 16 knights and ladies being personally chosen on the basis of their contribution to public and national life.

Every other year the knights and ladies of the Order, dressed in green velvet robes and white-plumed hats, process the short distance from the Signet Library in the centre of Edinburgh to the High Kirk of St Giles for a short service in the tiny Thistle Chapel, which was specially built in 1911. New knights are installed there by the sovereign and a further service follows in the main body of the Kirk, conducted by the Dean of the Thistle, a Church of Scotland minister who often, although not always, also holds the position of Dean of the Chapel Royal in Scotland.

November: National Service of Remembrance

The National Service of Remembrance is held every year at the Cenotaph on Whitehall, London, on the Sunday nearest to 11 November, the day in

1918 when the guns finally fell silent on the Western Front, signalling the end of the First World War. It commemorates the contribution and sacrifice of British and Commonwealth military and civilian servicemen and women in the two World Wars and later conflicts.

Its origins go back to 11 November 1920 when a single coffin, containing the body of the 'Unknown Warrior', travelled slowly by gun carriage from Victoria to Whitehall. The corpse had been chosen by the general officer commanding British troops in France and Flanders from six which had been exhumed from where they had fallen in Belgium by George Kendall, a Primitive Methodist minister who had become a British army chaplain partly at the suggestion of Queen Mary when she invited him to tea at Windsor Castle before the war after seeing him preaching in the street outside. The coffin, lined with zinc and made from an oak tree that had grown in Hampton Court Palace garden, was covered with a flag used as an altar cloth on the Western Front and a Crusader's sword from the Tower of London was placed inside it. The coffin plate bore the inscription: 'A British Warrior who fell in the Great War 1914 – 1918 for King and Country.'

As the procession carrying the coffin, led by the Massed Bands of the Household Division playing Chopin's Funeral March, neared Whitehall, King George V unveiled the newly built stone Cenotaph – the word means 'empty tomb'. Designed by Edwin Lutyens as a temporary structure for the 1919 Peace Day celebration, it proved to be so popular that a permanent replacement was constructed in Portland stone. At 10.50am a short service began there, the first National Act of Remembrance, before the

Unknown Warrior continued onwards to his final resting place inside Westminster Abbey.

Like most such events in the royal calendar, the service of remembrance follows the same course every year. It begins at precisely 10.36 am with a selection of national airs and solemn music, beginning with 'Rule Britannia!'. As the massed bands play Henry Purcell's 'Dido's Lament', the clergy led by a cross-bearer and the choir of the Chapel Royal process to their places by the Cenotaph. During *Solemn Melody* by Henry Walford Davies, politicians, high commissioners and representatives from different faiths assemble. The parade stands to attention in silence as the Royal Family emerge. As Big Ben strikes 11 a.m., the King's Troop Royal Horse Artillery fire a single shot salute from First World War-era guns on Horse Guards Parade. Two minutes' silence is observed and ended by a second gun salute and 'The Last Post' sounded by Royal Marines buglers.

The first wreath is laid on behalf of the nation by the sovereign with senior members of the royal family laying further wreaths, followed by service chiefs, politicians, and representatives of the Commonwealth and civilian services. The Bishop of London, as Dean of the Chapels Royal, leads a short Christian service of remembrance. At the end of the service the sovereign and other members of the Royal Family either salute or bow to the Cenotaph.

Late December: Christmas rose from Glastonbury

Each year about a week before Christmas a budded branch from the thorn tree in the churchyard of St John's Parish Church in Glastonbury is cut by the oldest pupil at St John's Infants School at a special ceremony led by the vicar and attended by the mayor and members of the town council. The thorn tree, a cutting from one which supposedly sprouted from Joseph of Arimathea's staff when he planted it on the nearby Wearyall hill, having come to Glastonbury with the Holy Grail, traditionally flowers on Christmas morning. The sprig is sent to the monarch to grace the royal family's festive table. During the ceremony, the children sing the 'Holy Thorn' song:

> There is a very special tree
> we call the holy thorn,
> that flowers in December,
> the month that Christ was born.
>
> We're told this very special tree
> grew from the staff of thorn,
> brought by a man called Joseph
> from the land where Christ was born.
>
> It now is our tradition
> to send a sprig of thorn
> to greet His Gracious Majesty
> on the day that Christ was born.

This ceremony seems to have originated in pre-Reformation times. Christmas cuttings were sent to Charles I and Charles II but the customs subsequently fell into abeyance. It was revived in 1929 by a vicar of Glastonbury whose sister-in-law was a lady in waiting to Queen Mary. It preserves a link between Arthurian legend and the modern British monarchy.

Christmas Day: The Christmas broadcast

It was John Reith, the sternly Presbyterian and fervently monarchist founding father of the BBC, who first conceived the idea of a royal Christmas broadcast. In 1932 he persuaded initially reluctant palace officials that George V should deliver a live Christmas Day message to the Empire. The broadcast from Sandringham, based on a script by Rudyard Kipling and introduced by a 65-year-old local shepherd, with carols and bell ringing from the local parish church choir, reached an estimated 20 million people in Australia, Canada, India, Kenya, South Africa, and the United Kingdom. Reith proudly recorded in his autobiography:

> It was the most spectacular success in BBC history thus far. The king had been heard all over the world with surprising clarity; only in New Zealand were parts of the speech inaudible owing to atmospherics. It was sensationally starred in foreign countries; the *New York Times* in large type: 'Distant lands thrill to his "God bless you"'; 2000 leading articles were counted in Broadcasting House.[1]

George V continued to make a live broadcast every Christmas Day until his death in 1936 when there was no royal broadcast. The tradition was nearly abandoned the following year when the Prime Minister, Neville Chamberlain, expressed the view that it was impossible for the monarch to come up with something new and interesting to say every year. 'How pathetic,' Reith characteristically noted in his diary, 'almost unbelievable. How typical of the attitude of politicians.'[2] He insisted that the broadcast become an annual fixture, as so it has remained. George VI overcame his stammer to deliver moving broadcasts throughout the Second World War which carried a strong Christian message clearly coming from the heart and made a deep impression on the millions who listened. On Christmas Day 1939, less than four months after the outbreak of the war, he famously said:

> I said to the man who stood at the Gate of the Year, 'Give me a light that I may tread safely into the unknown.' And he replied, 'Go out into the darkness, and put your hand into the hand of God. That shall be better to you than light, and safer than a known way.'[3]

Since it began as a live radio broadcast, the BBC has always transmitted the royal Christmas Day message at 3pm. This was originally chosen as the best time for reaching the countries of the Empire through short-wave radio transmitters from Britain. The transmission time was not changed when the Christmas broadcast moved to television in 1957 and from going out live to being recorded in 1960. The mid-afternoon slot has proved ideal for those at home rising from their festive lunch tables or preparing for a late afternoon or early evening meal. The monarch's broadcast regularly tops the Christmas Day television ratings – in 2021 it easily took top place, with a total audience across BBC and ITV of over 9 million; the next most watched programme, a *Strictly Come Dancing* Christmas Special had 5.8 million.

During the early decades of Elizabeth II's reign the broadcasts were often essentially glorified travelogues reflecting the places which members of the royal family had visited during the year. A radically new tone was introduced in 2000 when the Queen, speaking directly to camera, made testimony both to the importance of her own personal faith and to her sense of the importance of the spiritual dimension of life. 'For me', she said, 'the teachings of Christ and my own personal accountability before God provide a framework in which I try to lead my life. I, like so many of you, have drawn great comfort in difficult times from Christ's word and example.'

This particular message, which ended with the words of the blessing in the Book of Common Prayer which begins 'Go forth into the world in peace', attracted twenty five times more letters of appreciation to Buckingham Palace than any previous Christmas broadcast. It established a new role for the monarch speaking as a religious and spiritual leader as much as a head of state. As in subsequent broadcasts, while making very clear the strength of her own personal Christian conviction, the Queen also commended the teaching of other faiths, a theme that she frequently returned to in subsequent broadcasts (see pages 197–8).

Encouraged by the warm reception of the 2000 broadcast, and following her own personal instincts and those of her husband, the Queen maintained this strong personal religious tone through all of her subsequent Christmas broadcasts. In 2002, reflecting on a year that had seen the death of her mother and sister, she remarked 'I know just how much I rely on my own faith to guide me through the good times and the bad'. In subsequent broadcasts she retold the stories of several parables and made frequent references to specific teachings of Jesus while at the same time commending other faith perspectives and the British tradition of tolerance and religious pluralism. Christmas broadcasts in the latter years of her reign were often filmed in a church or a chapel rather than in the drawing-room setting that was for long the norm and ended with a prayer, quotation from the Bible or carol.

Charles III's first Christmas broadcast, delivered from the quire of St George's Chapel, Windsor on 25 December 2022, attracted an audience of 10.72 million, double that achieved by the next most popular Christmas Day television programme, *Strictly Come Dancing*, and the highest ever for a royal Christmas message. It very much followed the pattern and theme of his mother's later broadcasts with the chapel choir singing the National Anthem at the beginning and the carol 'O, little town of Bethlehem' at the end. The king spoke directly to camera about his own Christian faith and also warmly commended the other major world faiths, specifically mentioning the practical work of churches, synagogues, mosques, temples and gurdwaras in feeding the hungry and providing love and support to those in need.

The new king recalled his own visit to the Church of the Nativity in Bethlehem:

> There, I went down into the Chapel of the Manger and stood in silent reverence by the silver star that is inlaid on the floor and marks the place of our Lord Jesus Christ's birth. It meant more to me than I can possibly express to stand on that spot where, as the Bible tells us, 'The light that has come into the world' was born.

The new king went on to make much the same point that his mother had in her Easter broadcast in 2020 (page 201), concluding:

> While Christmas is, of course, a Christian celebration, the power of light overcoming darkness is celebrated across the boundaries of faith and belief. So, whatever faith you have, or whether you have none, it is in this life-giving light, and with the true humility that lies in our service to others, that I believe we can find hope for the future. Let us therefore celebrate it together, and cherish it always.

EPILOGUE

*The new king, his coronation and the sacred
nature of monarchy*

Charles III

The king who will be crowned and anointed on
6 May 2023 has a deep interest in religion and a
profound sense of the sacred. Throughout his adult
life he has manifested his passionate concern for the
spiritual through ways as various as his attachment
to the Book of Common Prayer and Authorized
Version of the Bible, his engagement with Orthodox
Christianity and Islam, his creation of a sacred
space known as The Sanctuary in the garden of his
home at Highgrove, Gloucestershire, and his public
championing of organic and sustainable agriculture,
holistic medicine and classical architecture. He has
pursued a personal crusade against the rising tide
of secular materialism and scientific reductionism.
Although official photographs often show him clad,
like previous princes, in military uniform or double-
breasted suit, he has also been caught on camera
garlanded while visiting a Hindu temple, dressed
in native fashion singing an eco-anthem in Guyana
or striding across a Hebridean island with a huge
shepherd's crook like a latter-day Columba.

In some ways this takes us back to the early
medieval model of king as philosopher and wise man.

Like Alfred, Charles has surrounded himself with advisers and spiritual counsellors and has a vision of spearheading national spiritual revival. In projects like the Prince's Trust and the revival of Dumfries House he has followed the more recent philanthropic tradition of welfare monarchy and emulated Prince Albert with his thirst for social improvement and determination to put his reforming principles into practice. At a deeper level, he harks back to a more primal understanding of the monarch as representing order and taking on the forces of chaos and, indeed, to the tragic, sacrificial dimension of royalty. A troubled and vulnerable figure, he has spoken often of the deep disintegration of the modern world and the need for it to be rebalanced and reordered. He himself has movingly expressed this driving passion in his life:

> I have gradually come to realise that my entire life so far has been motivated by a desire to heal – to heal the dismembered landscape and the poisoned soil; the cruelly shattered townscape, where harmony has been replaced by a cacophony; to heal the divisions between intuitive and rational thought, between mind, body and soul, so that the temple of our humanity can once again be lit by a sacred flame; to level the monstrous artificial barrier erected between tradition and modernity and, above all, to heal the mortally wounded soul that, alone, can give us warning of the folly of playing God and of believing that knowledge on its own is a substitute of wisdom.[1]

It is no coincidence that while Prince of Wales Charles made frequent appeals in his speeches to the concepts of wisdom and order so strongly associated with sacred kingship and Christian monarchy. In his 2000 Reith Lecture the word 'wisdom' figured seven times, coupled variously with the adjectives 'ancient', 'instinctive', 'practical' and 'intuitive'. He came back to this theme in 2109 at the time of the canonization of John Henry Newman, which he attended in Rome, praising the sense of harmony conveyed in Newman's poem, 'The Dream of Gerontius'. The appeal to order is very evident in a speech he made in 1996 extolling the virtues of tradition:

> Tradition is not a man-made element in our lives – it is a God-given awareness of the natural rhythms and of the fundamental harmony engendered by the paradoxical opposites in every aspect of nature. Tradition reflects the timeless order, and yet disorder, of the cosmos, and anchors us into a harmonious relationship with the great mysteries of the universe.[2]

For King Charles restoring order and harmony to our disintegrated world involves re-finding and reasserting a sense of the sacred. In 1996 he chose to speak to an audience of businessmen 'about a subject which I suspect is not often discussed on occasions like this – the importance of the sacred in the modern world'. His speech went on to lament the separation of science from religion and the separation of the natural world from God, 'with the result that it has fragmented the cosmos and placed the sacred into a separate, and secondary, compartment of our understanding, divorced from the practical day to day world of man'.[3] The need to rediscover a sense of the sacred in dealing with the natural world surfaced again in his reflection on the 2000 Reith Lectures which had explored the theme of sustainable development:

> If literally nothing is held sacred any more – because it is considered synonymous with superstition, or in some way 'irrational' – what is there to prevent us treating our entire world as some 'great laboratory of life', with potentially disastrous long-term consequences?
>
> Fundamentally, an understanding of the sacred helps us to acknowledge that there are bounds of balance, order and harmony in the natural world which set limits to our ambitions and define the parameters of sustainable development.[4]

Charles's 'Thought for the Day', broadcast on Radio 4 on 1 January 2000, made a heartfelt plea that 'in the new millennium we will begin to rediscover a sense of the sacred in all that surrounds us' and included a characteristic observation that 'it is a sacred thing to compose harmony out of opposites' as well as a commendation of the teaching of 'our Lord Jesus Christ ... that this life is but one passing phase of our existence'. [5] The fact that it was the heir to the throne rather than the Archbishop of Canterbury or some other church leader whom the BBC invited to give the first 'Thought for the Day' of the new millennium on the *Today* programme could be taken to indicate a recognition both of the continuing sacred dimension of monarchy and of Charles' particular religious interests. He also found himself nominated in a poll carried out for a Channel 4 programme in March 2001 as the third most powerful religious figure in Britain.

A striking example of this focus on the sacred has been the way in which Charles based his opposition to the genetic modification of plants on theological rather than scientific grounds.

> I happen to believe that this kind of genetic modification takes mankind into realms that belong to God, and to God alone...We live in an age of rights – it seems to me that it is time our Creator had some rights too.[6]

The columnist and broadcaster Libby Purves commented that many people would

> be outraged by the shameless fundamentalist way that the Prince brings God into the argument... Fashionably agnostic thinkers will be horribly annoyed that a pragmatic, rational argument should be defaced by this embarrassing mention of a creator with a capital 'C'. I was rather struck by it.[7]

Several academics did, indeed, object to the Prince's theological emphasis when dealing with what they took to be essentially neutral scientific topics. David Voas, a geographer at Liverpool University, complained that 'listening to the Prince of Wales is like going to church; having avoided it for a time you forget how dreadful it can be', and dismissed the heir to the throne as 'a self-indulgent preacher'.[8] The late Roman Catholic columnist, William Oddie, by contrast, saw the Prince's intervention in the GM debate as a welcome reassertion of royalty's traditional role 'as having an authority which was in some sense spiritual as well as temporal'.

The reason why Prince Charles is listened to on moral issues is twofold. Not only is the monarchy a more spiritual institution than we have come to suppose: we for our part are a more spiritual people.[9]

In a letter to *The Times* I concurred with this analysis and took it further:

At a time when its constitutional role is coming increasingly into question, I suspect that the spiritual dimension of monarchy may come to assume increasing importance.

In his stand against genetically modified crops, Prince Charles has shown himself not so much the defender of faiths as the supreme exponent of an essentially religious perspective on life in the prevailing climate of secular and scientific rationalism.[10]

The strongly spiritual perspective introduced by Charles as Prince of Wales into discussions about contemporary issues had a greater appeal abroad than it did to church leaders at home. On a visit to Guyana in 2000, he was singled out for commendation by the mayor of Georgetown who prayed: 'I ask the Creator to give you the strength and wisdom to remain in the vanguard helping keep the world safe, clean, good and green'.[11] In 2002 a statue was erected in the Brazilian town of Palmas in the middle of the Amazonian rain forest depicting him as an angel and, in the words of the local state governor 'saving the world.' It shows the prince, with wings outstretched, hovering over a sea of humanity with his arms in open embrace. For leaders of the Church of England, by contrast, his attitudes were rather confused. As Archbishop of Canterbury, Robert Runcie apparently found him a mass of confusions and contradictions in respect of religion, one moment extolling the 'epic language of the Prayer Book' and the next 'exploring Hinduism with people in the inner cities.' [12]

As king, Charles will not have the same freedom to speak out on issues about which he feels passionately as he did while heir to the throne and he has indicated that he understands the constraints of monarchy in this regard. It seems unlikely, however, that he will lose his commitment to the sacred and his lifelong spiritual quest. In contrast to the more sure, settled and measured faith of his late mother, he has a restless, questing spirituality combined with a love of tradition, while sharing her emphasis on harmony, forgiveness and reconciliation. In this, he is close to what a lot of people in Britain feel. This was well expressed in comments made to the *Washington Post* by Andi Britt, who came with his wife to place flowers in front of Buckingham Palace in memory of Queen Elizabeth following her death: 'He represents those people who perhaps don't have a vibrant faith, but have a sense that there is a loving God. He represents a faith and a God who welcomes people, regardless of how close they feel. I think he represents many people who are just not as sure, or who don't have such strong convictions — people of faith, different faiths, or no faith.' [13]

The Coronation and the Sacred Nature of Monarchy

This book has surveyed the primal, biblical basis of sacred kingship, the history of Christian monarchy in Britain and the roles and responsibilities that traditionally go with it. All these are crystallised, concentrated and expressed in richly symbolic form in the coronation service. For what will Charles III be set apart, anointed, consecrated and blessed on 6 May 2023? First and foremost to act as a focus for unity in an increasingly fragmented and polarised nation. The official definition of the sovereign's role, as expressed by the Government, is to be 'the living symbol of national unity'.[14] The extent to which the monarchy now bears this weighty role almost single-handed was well expressed by John Habgood, when Archbishop of York:

> There is not a single free nation in the world which has managed to hold a pluralist society together without some very powerful unifying factor. In Britain, we used to have a whole network of such factors mostly linked in some way to the Church and Crown. One of the effects of the decline of the national role of the Church has been to isolate the Crown as almost the only effective symbol of national unity. [15]

Among the most important ways in which monarchy promotes unity is by emphasizing the communal over against the individualistic. Writing about the development of sacred kingship, the sociologist Werner Stark has observed that:

> The societies in which the monarchical religion flourished were, by and large, communities … they were unities rather than diversities; they were collectivistic rather than individualistic; the whole was before the parts, both in reality

and evaluation. This unity, this collectivism, this primacy of the whole needed to be made visible, to be symbolized, and its visible image, its commanding symbol, was the sacred king.[16]

Stark goes on to say that societies ditched their monarchs when they ceased to be communal and became associational. One might well reflect that is a wonder we have held on to our monarchy so long in Britain, when privatisation and selfish, competitive individualism are so much in the ascendant. This is precisely why we need the monarchy. It cannot stand alone and Canute-like against the tide but it can symbolise a commitment to public service and to communal rather than private interest. Elizabeth II and Charles III have both embodied and expressed a unifying, communal ethic. In the Queen's case, it was demonstrated both through her 'one nation' perspective and in her very strong personal commitment to the Commonwealth and the principles underlying it. In the case of Charles, whose overriding ideology has been characterised by his biographer James Morton as 'communitarian', it has been in the fostering through both speeches and practical philanthropic activities of an ethic of mutual obligation and co-operation and a sense of belonging.[17]

The sense of unity which the monarchy symbolises, and which it can indeed help to engender, has a particular spiritual dimension. It was particularly evident in the aftermath of the late Queen's death, as evidenced and discussed in the introduction to this book. It also shows itself in those occasions which come closest to expressing a shared collective sense of national identity – Remembrance Day celebrations, royal weddings and funerals, ceremonies to commemorate significant anniversaries and major tragedies involving significant loss of life. These events share three characteristics. They involve religious services, they acknowledge in their different ways the transcendent and spiritual dimension of life, and they are graced by the presence of the monarch and other members of the royal family. It is the royal presence, almost as much as their liturgical context and content, which helps to establish their spiritual as well as their national atmosphere and resonance. The monarchy does, indeed, in a very real sense, enshrine the soul of our country.

There is another more specifically religious dimension to the monarchy's role in promoting unity that King Charles recognised when he spoke in 2017 at the Oxford Centre for Islamic Studies:

> We need to rediscover and explore what unites rather than what divides us. And that involves a recognition that we have all learned from each other and should continue to do so. No one culture contains the complete truth. We are all seekers. And our search is – or should be – a collective human enterprise.[18]

Those words, which reflect the king's own spiritual quest and his desire to be Defender of Faith, perhaps hint at a new spiritual and sacred role for monarchy. It has traditionally stood for values like loyalty, service, duty and self-sacrifice. It perhaps also increasingly stands for another set of values – healing, wholeness, openness, tolerance and vulnerability.

Might it be, indeed, that the monarchy can best contribute to social cohesion, shared values and the development of a renewed generous national identity in a multi-faith and multicultural society by being re-sacralised and emphasizing its sacred and spiritual nature? In our cynical, selfish and secular society there is considerable doubt and debate as to the future of monarchy in general and Christian monarchy in particular. Most recent defences of monarchy and calls for its reform have advocated an essentially secular model. This book has sought to put forward the counter-cultural proposition that it still has a vital role and that this role is primarily sacred. It involves symbolising and embodying spiritual values, representing and defending religious faith against unbelief and secular materialism, promoting order in the midst of chaos, assisting the recovery of our lost metaphysical imagination, standing for the public good against private gain and acting as a focal point for unity in a society which is increasingly fragmented and fissiparous.

Ultimately, monarchy points beyond itself to the majesty, mystery and vulnerability of God. It is a lonely, noble, sacrificial calling. What our sovereign needs and deserves most is our loyal and heartfelt prayers. As we prepare for the king's coronation, we could do well to reflect on and respond to the request that his mother made before hers:

> You will be keeping it as a holiday; but I want to ask you all, whatever your religion maybe, to pray for me on that day, to pray that God may give me wisdom and strength to carry out the solemn promises I shall be making, and that I may faithfully serve them and you, all the days of my life.

God save the King!

NOTES

The place of publication of all books cited is London unless otherwise stated.

Introduction

1 'Britain might not be as secular as we thought', *Credo* column, *The Times*, 17 September 2022

2 Walter Bagehot, *The English Constitution* (Oxford World's Classics, 2001), pp.41, 45

3 Paul Theroux, *The Kingdom by the Sea* (Penguin Books, 1983), p.257

4 Anne Rowbottom, 'Royal Symbolism and Social Integration' (PhD thesis, University of Manchester, 1994); 'The Real Royalists: Folk Performance and Civil Religion at Royal Visits', *Folklore*, 109 (1998)

5 Ben Pimlott, *The Queen* (HarperCollins, 2001), p.210

6 Stephen Bates, *The Shortest History of the Crown* (Old Street Publishing, 2022), p.123

7 Walter Walsh, *The Religious Life and Influence of Queen Victoria* (Swan Sonnenschein, 1902), p.184

8 'Should Queen Elizabeth II be made a saint?', *Spectator,* 24 September 2022; letters in *The Tablet* from Graham Rhys-Jones & Alan Pavelin, 24 September 2022; letter in *The Times* from Rev Peter Wolton, 20 September 2022

9 Frank Prochaska, *Royal Bounty: The Making of a Welfare Monarchy* (Penguin, 1995)

Chapter 1

1 J. Frazer, *The Golden Bough* (Macmillan, 1987), p. 20.

2 *Ibid.*, p. 91.

3 J. Carey, 'Ideal Kingship in Early Ireland' in *Monarchy* (Temenos Academy, 2002), p. 51.

4 G. Lindop, 'The wheel turning monarch: An ideal of kingship in early Buddhism', *Monarchy* (Temenos Academy, 2002), p. 117.

5 K. Raine, 'Monarchy and the Imagination' in *Monarchy* (Temenos Academy, 2002), pp.20-21.

6 R. Moore and D. Gillette, *The King Within* (Avon Books, New York, 1992), p. 110.

NOTES

7   *Ibid.*, p.105.

Chapter 2

1   This subject is discussed much more fully in my book *God is Green* (Darton, Longman and Todd, 2020)

2   H. Frankfort, *Kingship and the Gods* (University of Chicago Press, 1944), pp.3, 12

3   O. O'Donovan, *The Desire of Nations* (Cambridge University Press, 1996), p.61

Chapter 3

1   O. O'Donovan, *The Desire of Nations* (Cambridge University Press, 1996), p.123

Chapter 4

1   *Bede, Ecclesiastical History of the English People* (Oxford World's Classics, 1999), p.59

2   Adomnán of Iona, *Life of St Columba* (Penguin Books, 1991), p.120

3   G. Ashe, *King Arthur's Avalon* (Fontana, 1990), p. 241

4   S. Keys and M. Lapidge (eds.), *Asser's Life of King Alfred* (Penguin, 1983), p. 91

5   D. Baldwin, *The Chapel Royal* (Duckworth, 1990), p. 18

6   E. H. Kantorowicz, *The King's Two Bodies* (Princeton University Press, Princeton, New Jersey, 1957), pp. 56, 49

Chapter 5

1   H .G. Reventlow, *The Authority of the Bible and the Rise of the Modern World* (SCM Press, 1984), pp.136-7

2   J. Craigie (ed.), *The Basilikon Doron of King James VI* (Scottish Text Society, Edinburgh, 1944), Vol. I, p. 75

3   W. Stark, *The Sociology of Religion* (Routledge and Kegan Paul, 1966), Vol. I, pp. 65-6

4   A. Nicolson, *Power and Glory: Jacobean England and the Making of the King James Bible* (Harper Perennial, 2004), p. xviii

5   J. B. Torrance, 'The Covenant Concept in Scottish Theology and Politics and its Legacy', *Scottish Journal of Theology*, Vol. 34 (1981), p.238

6   John, 3rd Marquess of Bute, *Scottish Coronations* (Alex Gardner, Paisley, 1902) p. 173.

7   F. Prochaska, *Royal Bounty: The Making of a Welfare Monarchy* (Yale University Press, New Haven, 1995), p. 6

8   O'Donovan, *Desire of Nations*, pp. 240-1

9   H. More, 'Daniel', *Sacred Dramas* (1782), p. 241

10 W. Walsh, *The Religious Life of Queen Victoria* (Swan Sonnenschein, 1902), p.258

11 W. Bagehot, *The English Constitution*, World's Classics edn. (Oxford University Press, Oxford, 1928), pp.39, 40

12 *Ibid.*,p.47

13 D. Cannadine, 'The Context, Performance and Meaning of Ritual: The British Monarchy and the Invention of Tradition, c.1820-1977' in E. Hobsbawm and T. Ranger (eds.), *The Invention of Tradition* (Cambridge University Press, 1992)

14 J.Wolffe, *God and Greater Britain* (Routledge, 1994), p. 155

15 P. Brendon and P. Whitehead, *The Windsors. A Dynasty Revealed* (Hodder and Stoughton, 1994), p. 27

16 D. Marquand, *Ramsay Macdonald* (Cape, 1977), p. 774

17 *The Times,* 11 May 1937

18 J. Wolffe, *Great Deaths* (Oxford University Press, Oxford, 2001), p. 6

Chapter 6

1   M. Enright, *Iona, Tara and Soissons: The Origin of the Royal Anointing Ritual* (Walter de Gruyter, Berlin, 1985), p. 75.

2   T. Silver, *The Coronation Service or Consecration of the Anglo-Saxon Kings* (Oxford, 1831), pp .22, 23

3   N. F. Cantor, *Church, Kingship and Lay Investiture in England 1089-1135* (Princeton University Press, 1958), p.191

4   J. Perkins, *Crowning the Sovereign* (Methuen, 1937), p.49

5   R. Strong, *Coronation* (HarperCollins, 2005), pp.170-1

6   G. Reedy, 'Mystical Politics: The Imagery of Charles II's Coronation' in P. J. Korshin ed., *Studies in Change and Revolution* (Scolar Press, Aldershot, 1972), pp.19-42

7   J. Cannon and R. Griffiths, *The Oxford Illustrated History of the British Monarchy* (Oxford University Press, Oxford, 1997), p. 29.

8   *Ibid.*, p. 608

Chapter 7

1   *The Form and Order of Service for the Coronation of Her Majesty Queen Elizabeth II* (Eyre and Spottiswoode, 1953), p. 4

2   *Ibid.*, p. 8-9

NOTES

3 J. Perkins, *The Crowning of the Sovereign* (Methuen, 1937), p. 60

4 *Service for the Coronation of Elizabeth II*, p.23

5 *Ibid.*, p.23

6 *Ibid.*, p.24

7 *Ibid*, p.24

8 R. Strong, *Coronation*, p.227

9 *Service for the Coronation of Elizabeth II*, p.28

10 *Ibid.*, p.29

11 R. Morris, 'The Coronation of Charles III', (Constitution Unit, University College, London, 2022), p.37

12 *Daily Telegraph*, 12 October 2022; *Herald*, 12 October 2022

13 C. Pepinster, *Defender of the Faith: The British Monarchy, Religion and the Next Coronation* (Hodder & Stoughton, 2022), p.267

14 *The Coronation Of Their Majesties King George VI and Queen Elizabeth*. Official Souvenir Programme (Oldhams Press, 1937), p.22

Chapter 8

1 Quoted in G. Reedy, 'Mystical Politics: The Imagery of Charles II's Coronation' in P. J. Korshin (ed.), *Studies in Change and Revolution* (Scolar Press, Aldershot, 1972), p.19

2 W. Walsh, *The Religious Life of Queen Victoria* (Swan Sonnenschein, 1902), p. 16

3 Mike Priestley, 'Not-so-blunt words that stopped a Coronation', *Bradford Telegraph and Argus*, 1 December 2006

4 *The Times,* 12 May 1937

5 K. Harris, *The Queen* (Orion, 1994), p.145

6 K. Martin, *The Crown and the Establishment* (Hutcheson, 1962), p.19

7 Lord Altrincham, *Is the Monarchy Perfect?* (John Calder, 1958), p.11

8 *Daily Telegraph*, 29 June 1994

9 J. Paxman, *On Royalty* (Viking, 2006), pp.125, 127, 130

10 *Ibid.*, pp. 283-4

11 E. Shils and M. Young, 'The Meaning of the Coronation', *Sociological Review*, New Series, Vol.1 (1953), p.67

12 *Ibid.,* p.65

13 *Ibid.*, p.79

14 *Ibid.*, p.67

15 *Ibid.*, p.71

16 *Ibid.*, p.80
17 *Ibid.*, p.68

Chapter 9

1 K. H. Brown, *The Records of the Parliaments of Scotland to 1707* (St Andrews, 2007-16), 1689/6/6

2 Quoted by C. Pepinster, *Defender of the Faith*, p.68

3 E. A. Smith, *George IV* (New Haven: Yale University Press, 1999), p.239

4 Walsh, *The Religious Life of Queen Victoria*, p.214

5 Quoted in A. Leak, 'Listening to them but not liking them – Queen Victoria's bishops', *Church Times*, 19 January 2001, p.17.

6 A. Ponsonby, *H. Ponsonby, Queen Victoria's Private Secretary, His Life from His Letters* (Macmillan, 1942), p. 178

7 M. Bloch, *The Reign and Abdication of Edward VIII* (Black Swan, 1991), pp.34-5

8 *Church Times*, 30 May 2003, p.17

9 Swearing in the New King', Constitution Unit, May 2018, p.20

10 The Royal Accession and Coronation Oaths, Constitution Unit, October 2016, p.6

Chapter 10

1 O. Chadwick, *The Victorian Church*, 2nd edn. (A & C Black, 1980),Vol. II, p. 336

2 *Ibid.*, p. 33

3 Quoted in K. Harris, *The Queen*, pp. 373-4

4 *The Tablet*, 2 February 2002, p. 19

5 P. Avis, *Church, State and Establishment* (SPCK, 2001), pp. 29-30

6 Quoted in R. A. Mason (ed.), *John Knox and the British Reformations* (Ashgate, Aldershot,1998), p. 174

7 T. McCrie, *Life of Andrew Melville* (William Blackwood, Edinburgh, 1824),Vol.I, p. 92

8 W. Walsh, *The Religious Life of Queen Victoria* (Swan Sonnenschein, 1902), p.29

9 A. Ponsonby, *H. Ponsonby, Queen Victoria's Private Secretary, His Life from His Letters* (Macmillan, 1942), p. 118

10 Walsh, *Religious Life of Queen Victoria*, p. 33

11 *Ibid.*, p. 32

NOTES

12 Quoted in A. Leak, 'Listening to them but not liking them – Queen Victoria's bishops', *Church Times*, 19 January 2001, p.17

13 I. Bradley, 'Partial to Presbyterianism', *Life and Work*, January 2001, p.15.

14 Walsh, *Religious Life of Queen Victoria*, p.260

15 A. Leask, 'Listening to them', p.17

16 C. Pepinster, *Defenders of the Faith*, p.112

17 *Ibid.*, p.234

18 Email to author, 15 September 2022

Chapter 11

1 *Religious Discrimination Project: Interim Report* (University of Derby, 2000), p. 80

2 C. Pepinster, *Defenders of the Faith*, p.150

3 C. Longley, *Chosen People: Anglo-American Myth and Reality* (Hodder and Stoughton, London, 2002), pp. 20-1

4 Aleem Maqbool, 'How the Queen's Christian faith went beyond duty', BBC News website, 18 September 2022, https://www.bbc.co.uk/news/uk-62942772

5 *Ibid.*

6 'A Speech by the Queen at Lambeth Palace', 15 February 2012, https://www.royal.uk/queens-speech-lambeth-palace-15-february-2012

7 'Beyond Belief: Prince Philip', BBC Radio 4, 12 April 2021, https://www.bbc.co.uk/programmes/m000v1nx

8 J. Dimbleby, *The Prince of Wales: A Biography* (Little, Brown, 1994), p. 52

9 *Ibid.*

10 *Ibid.*

11 *Sunday Times*, 26 June 1994

12 Dimbleby, *Prince of Wales*, p. 528

13 Harriet Sherwood, 'Monarch will aim to protect all UK faiths', *Guardian*, 10 September 2022

14 Kevin Sullivan, 'King Charles III may bring new approach to "Defender of the Faith"', *Washington Post*, 13 September 2022

15 'The King's remarks to Faith Leaders', 16 September 2022, https://www.royal.uk/kings-remarks-faith-leaders

16 Speech at King Hussein's memorial service, 5 July 1999

GOD SAVE THE KING

17 R. Hazell & B. Morris (eds.), *The Role of Monarchy in Modern Democracy* (Oxford: Hart Publishing, 2020), p.96
18 Letter to *The Times*, 1 December 2022

Chapter 12
1 J. Reith, *Into the Wind* (Hodder and Stoughton, 1949), p. 169
2 C. Stuart, *The Reith Diaries* (Collins, 1975), p. 197
3 *King George VI to His Peoples 1936-51. Selected Broadcasts and Speeches* (John Murray, 1952), p.21

Epilogue
1 'A Time to Heal', *Temenos* 5 (Spring 2003), p.15
2 'The Sacred in Modern Life'. Speech to the Investcorp Dinner, 10 July 1996
3 *Ibid.*
4 'A Reflection on the 2000 Reith Lectures'. BBC Radio 4, 17 May 2000
5 'Thought for the Day', BBC Radio 4, 1 January 2000
6 'Seeds of Disaster', *Daily Telegraph*, 8 June 1998
7 'Of cabbages and princes', *The Times*, 9 June 1998
8 *Higher Calling* (Journal of Values in Higher Education), No.4 (June 2000), p.17
9 W. Oddie, 'Royal authority, both temporal and spiritual', *The Times*, 12 June 1999
10 *The Times*, 17 June 1999
11 *Daily Telegraph*, 26 February 2000
12 H. Carpenter, *Robert Runcie* (Hodder and Stoughton, 1996), pp. 220-5
13 Kevin Sullivan, 'King Charles III may bring new approach to "Defender of the Faith"', *Washington Post*, 13 September 2022
14 *The Monarchy in Britain* (Central Office of Information, 1983), p. 10
15 J. Habgood, *Church and Nation in a Secular Age* (Darton, Longman and Todd, 1983), p. 30
16 W. Stark, *The Sociology of Religion*, Vol.1 (Routledge, Kegan and Paul, 1966), p.136
17 J. Morton, *Prince Charles – Breaking the Cycle* (Ebury Press, 1998), pp. 265-6
18 Speech by HRH Prince of Wales, 16 May 2017